To Be Found Faithful

A Study of 2nd Timothy

Will you make the choice to live faithfully to
your God every day?

MELANIE NEWTON

JOYFUL
WALK
BIBLE
STUDIES

We extend our heartfelt thanks to the many women who served as contributors to the original study guide in 1999, especially Liz Church, Lori Schweers, Joan Floyd, and Penny Semmelbeck. Thanks also to Marlo Brazeal, Susan Lewis, Julia Gendron, Marlyn Scott, and Pam Lovell who helped me to update and revise this study in 2019. We appreciate your input.

To Be Found Faithful: A Study of 2nd Timothy

© 2025 Melanie Newton. All rights reserved.

Published by Joyful Walk Press. Flower Mound, TX

ISBN: 979-8-9925303-8-4

For questions about the use of this study guide or for bulk orders please email us at melanienewton.com/contact.

Cover graphic adapted from plouzane-1758197_1920.jpg, a public domain image accessed at pixabay.com.

Melanie Newton is the author of "Graceful Beginnings" books for anyone new to the Bible and "Joyful Walk Bible Studies" for established Christians. Her mission is to help women learn to study the Bible for themselves and to grow their Bible-teaching skills to lead others.

Joyful Walk Bible Studies are grace-based studies for women of all ages. Each study guide follows the inductive method of Bible study (observation, interpretation, application) in a warm and inviting format.

We pray that you and your group will find *To Be Found Faithful* a resource that God will use to strengthen you in your faith walk with God.

Christ-Focused • Grace-Based • Bible-Rich

JOYFUL WALK PRESS
Flower Mound, TX

MELANIE NEWTON

Melanie Newton is a Louisiana girl who made the choice to follow Jesus while attending LSU. She and her husband Ron married and moved to Texas for him to attend Dallas Theological Seminary. They stayed in Texas where Ron led a wilderness camping ministry for troubled youth for many years. Ron now helps corporations with their challenging employees and is the author of the top-rated business book, *No Jerks on the Job*.

Melanie jumped into raising three Texas-born children and serving in ministry to women at her church. Through the years, the Lord has given her opportunity to do Bible teaching and to write grace-based Bible studies for women that are now available from her website (melanienewton.com) and on Bible.org. *Graceful Beginnings* books are for anyone new to the Bible. *Joyful Walk Bible Studies* are for maturing Christians.

Melanie is a speaker, author, and trainer with Joyful Walk Ministries. Her mission is to help women learn to study the Bible for themselves and to grow their Bible-teaching skills to lead others. Her heart's desire is to encourage you to have a joyful relationship with Jesus Christ so you are willing to share that experience with others around you.

"Jesus took hold of me in 1972, and I've been on this great adventure ever since. My life is a gift of God, full of blessings in the midst of difficult challenges. The more I've learned and experienced God's absolutely amazing grace, the more I've discovered my faith walk to be a joyful one. I'm still seeking that joyful walk every day..."

Melanie

OTHER BIBLE STUDIES BY MELANIE NEWTON

Download our catalogue and get resources for your spiritual growth at melanienewton.com.

Graceful Beginnings Series books for anyone new to the Bible:

A Fresh Start (basics for new Christians)

Painting the Portrait of Jesus (the Gospel of John)

The God You Can Know (the character of God)

Grace Overflowing (an overview of Paul's 13 letters)

The Walk from Fear to Faith (7 Old Testament women)

Satisfied by His Love (women who knew Jesus)

Seek the Treasure (study of Ephesians)

Pathways to a Joyful Walk (6 pathways to a joy-filled life)

Songs of the Heart That Light My Way (selected Psalms)

Joyful Walk Bible Studies for growing Christians:

Adorn Yourself with Godliness (1 Timothy and Titus, also in Spanish)

Everyday Women, Ever Faithful God (Old Testament women, also in Spanish)

Connecting Faith to Sight (Genesis 1-11)

Graceful Living (the essentials for a grace-based Christian life)

Graceful Living Today (a devotional journal for a joyful life)

Healthy Living (Colossians and Philemon)

Heartbreak to Hope (the Gospel of Mark)

Identity: Sticking to Your Faith in a Pull-Apart World (Ezra thru Malachi)

Knowing Jesus, Knowing Joy (Philippians, also in Spanish)

Live Out His Love (New Testament women)

Perspective (1and 2 Thessalonians)

Profiles of Perseverance (Old Testament men, also in Spanish)

Radical Acts (Acts)

Reboot, Renew, Rejoice (1 and 2 Chronicles)

The God-Dependent Woman (2 Corinthians)

To Be Found Faithful (2 Timothy)

Resources for leading others

Be a Christ-Focused Small Group Leader

Leap into Lifestyle Disciplemaking

Painting the Picture of Jesus (the "I Am's" of Jesus lessons for children)

Teaching Children the God They Can Know (the character of God for children)

CONTENTS

Using This Study Guide 1

Paul's Second Letter to Timothy 3

1: Truth and Faithfulness 9

2: Stay Faithful without Fear 19

3: Faithfulness without Shame 29

4: The Hard Work of Faithfulness 39

5: Faith-Building Words 51

6: Influential Fakers 61

7: A Faithful Life with No Regrets 73

8: Stay Faithful to the End 85

Kindle Your Spiritual Gifts 95

Small Group Discussion Guide 97

Sources 107

Using This Study Guide

This study guide consists of 8 lessons covering the last letter in our New Testament written by the Apostle Paul—2ⁿᵈ Timothy.

The lessons are divided into 4 sections (about 20 minutes in length). The first 3 sections contain a detail study of the passages. The last section is a podcast that provides additional insight to the lesson.

If you cannot do the entire lesson one week, please read the Bible passage covered by the lesson and try to do the "Day One Study" of the lesson.

THE BASIC STUDY

Each lesson includes core questions covering the passage narrative. These core questions will take you through the process of inductive Bible study—observation, interpretation, and application. It is the best approach for doing Bible Study. The process is more easily understood in the context of answering these questions:

- What does the passage say? (**Observation**: what's actually there)
- What does it mean? (**Interpretation**: the author's intended meaning)
- How does this apply to me today? (**Application**: making it personal)

STUDY ENHANCEMENTS

Study Aids: To aid in proper interpretation and application of the study, five additional study aids are located where appropriate in the lesson:

- Historical Insight
- Scriptural Insight
- From the Greek (definitions of Greek words)
- Focus on the Meaning
- Think About It (thoughtful reflection)
- Dependent Living (relying on Christ)

Other useful study tools: Use online tools or apps (blueletterbible.org or "Blue Letter Bible app" is especially helpful) to find *cross references* (verses with similar content to what you are studying) and meanings of the *original Greek words or phrases* used (usually called "interlinear"). You can also look at any verse in *various Bible translations* to help with understanding what it is saying. Soniclight.com and gotquestions.org are also reliable resources to use. Feel free to add your own study at the end of each lesson.

PODCASTS

Find podcasts for these lessons at melanienewton.com/2-timothy and most podcast providers. Or you can read the blogs associated with the podcasts at melanienewton.com/blog. Choose 2 Timothy category then scroll to find the title you want. Listen to the first podcast as an introduction to the study.

NEW TESTAMENT SUMMARY

The New Testament opens with the births of Jesus and John (often called "the baptist"). About 30 years later, John challenged the Jews to indicate their repentance (turning from sin and toward God) by submitting to water baptism—a familiar Old Testament practice used for repentance as well as when a Gentile converted to Judaism (to be washed clean of idolatry).

Jesus, God's incarnate Son, publicly showed the world what God is like and taught His perfect ways for 3 – 3½ years. After preparing 12 disciples to continue Christ's earthly work, He died voluntarily on a cross for mankind's sin, rose from the dead, and returned to heaven. The account of His earthly life is recorded in 4 books known as the Gospels (the biblical books of Matthew, Mark, Luke and John named after the compiler of each account).

After Jesus' return to heaven, the followers of Christ were then empowered by the Holy Spirit and spread God's salvation message among the Jews, a number of whom believed in Christ. The apostle Paul and others carried the good news to the Gentiles during 3 missionary journeys (much of this recorded in the book of Acts). Paul wrote 13 New Testament letters to churches & individuals (Romans through Philemon). The section in our Bible from Hebrews to Jude contains 8 additional letters penned by five men, including two apostles (Peter and John) and two of Jesus' half-brothers (James and Jude). The author of Hebrews is unknown. The apostle John also recorded Revelation, which summarizes God's final program for the world. The Bible ends as it began—with a new, sinless creation.

DISCUSSION GROUP GUIDELINES

1. **Attend consistently** whether your lesson is done or not. You'll learn from the other women, and they want to get to know you.

2. **Set aside time** to work through the study questions. The goal of Bible study is to **get to know** Jesus. He will change your life.

3. **Share your insights** from your personal study time. As you spend time in the Bible, Jesus will teach you truth through His Spirit inside you.

4. **Respect each other's insights**. Listen thoughtfully. Encourage each other as you interact. Refrain from dominating the discussion if you have a tendency to be talkative. ☺

5. **Celebrate our unity** in Christ. Avoid bringing up controversial subjects such as politics, divisive issues, and denominational differences.

6. **Maintain confidentiality.** Remember that anything shared during the group time is not to leave the **group** (unless permission is granted by the one sharing).

7. **Pray for one another** as sisters in Christ.

8. **Get to know the women** in your group. Please do not use your small group members for solicitation purposes for home businesses, though.

There is a small group discussion guide available at the end of this study. Anyone can use the guide to lead a group through a discussion of the questions in this study. This is especially useful for groups that have less than two hours to meet together.

Enjoy your Joyful Walk Bible Study!

Paul's Second Letter to Timothy

New International Version (2011)

Paul, an apostle of Christ Jesus by the will of God, in keeping with the promise of life that is in Christ Jesus,

To Timothy, my dear son: Grace, mercy and peace from God the Father and Christ Jesus our Lord.

I thank God, whom I serve, as my ancestors did, with a clear conscience, as night and day I constantly remember you in my prayers. Recalling your tears, I long to see you, so that I may be filled with joy. I am reminded of your sincere faith, which first lived in your grandmother Lois and in your mother Eunice and, I am persuaded, now lives in you also. For this reason I remind you to fan into flame the gift of God, which is in you through the laying on of my hands. For the Spirit God gave us does not make us timid, but gives us power, love and self-discipline.

So do not be ashamed of the testimony about our Lord or of me his prisoner. Rather, join with me in suffering for the gospel, by the power of God. He has saved us and called us to a holy life—not because of anything we have done but because of his own purpose and grace. This grace was given us in Christ Jesus before the beginning of time, but it has now been revealed through the appearing of our Savior, Christ Jesus, who has destroyed death and has brought life and immortality to light through the gospel. And of this gospel I was appointed a herald and an apostle and a teacher. That is why I am suffering as I am. Yet this is no cause for shame, because I know whom I have believed, and am convinced that he is able to guard what I have entrusted to him until that day.

What you heard from me, keep as the pattern of sound teaching, with faith and love in Christ Jesus. Guard the good deposit that was entrusted to you—guard it with the help of the Holy Spirit who lives in us.

You know that everyone in the province of Asia has deserted me, including Phygelus and Hermogenes.

May the Lord show mercy to the household of Onesiphorus, because he often refreshed me and was not ashamed of my chains. On the contrary, when he was in Rome, he searched hard for me until he found me. May the Lord grant that he will find mercy from the Lord on that day! You know very well in how many ways he helped me in Ephesus.

You then, my son, be strong in the grace that is in Christ Jesus. And the things you have heard me say in the presence of many witnesses entrust to reliable people who will also be qualified to teach others. Join with me in suffering, like a good soldier of Christ Jesus. No one serving as a soldier gets entangled in civilian affairs, but rather tries to please his commanding officer. Similarly, anyone who competes as an athlete does not receive the victor's crown except by competing according to the rules. The hardworking farmer should be the first to receive a share of the crops. Reflect on what I am saying, for the Lord will give you insight into all this.

Remember Jesus Christ, raised from the dead, descended from David. This is my gospel, for which I am suffering even to the point of being chained like a criminal. But God's word is not chained. Therefore I endure everything for the sake of the elect, that they too may obtain the salvation that is in Christ Jesus, with eternal glory.

Here is a trustworthy saying:

If we died with him, we will also live with him; if we endure, we will also reign with him. If we disown him, he will also disown us; if we are faithless, he remains faithful, for he cannot disown himself.

Keep reminding God's people of these things. Warn them before God against quarreling about words; it is of no value, and only ruins those who listen. Do your best to present yourself to God as one approved, a worker who does not need to be ashamed and who correctly handles the word of truth. Avoid godless chatter, because those who indulge in it will become more and more ungodly. Their teaching will spread like gangrene. Among them are Hymenaeus and Philetus, who have departed from the truth. They say that the resurrection has already taken place, and they destroy the faith of some. Nevertheless, God's solid foundation stands firm, sealed with this inscription: "The Lord knows those who are his," and, "Everyone who confesses the name of the Lord must turn away from wickedness."

In a large house there are articles not only of gold and silver, but also of wood and clay; some are for special purposes and some for common use. Those who cleanse themselves from the latter will be instruments for special purposes, made holy, useful to the Master and prepared to do any good work.

Flee the evil desires of youth and pursue righteousness, faith, love and peace, along with those who call on the Lord out of a pure heart. Don't have anything to do with foolish and stupid arguments, because you know they produce quarrels. And the Lord's servant must not be quarrelsome but must be kind to everyone, able to teach, not resentful. Opponents must be gently instructed, in the hope that God will grant them repentance leading them to a knowledge of the truth, and that they will come to their senses and escape from the trap of the devil, who has taken them captive to do his will.

But mark this: There will be terrible times in the last days. People will be lovers of themselves, lovers of money, boastful, proud, abusive, disobedient to their parents, ungrateful, unholy, without love, unforgiving, slanderous, without self-control, brutal, not lovers of the good, treacherous, rash, conceited, lovers of pleasure rather than lovers of God— having a form of godliness but denying its power. Have nothing to do with such people.

They are the kind who worm their way into homes and gain control over gullible women, who are loaded down with sins and are swayed by all kinds of evil desires, always learning but never able to come to a knowledge of the truth. Just as Jannes and Jambres opposed Moses, so also these teachers oppose the truth. They are men of depraved minds, who, as far as the faith is concerned, are rejected. But they will not get very far because, as in the case of those men, their folly will be clear to everyone.

You, however, know all about my teaching, my way of life, my purpose, faith, patience, love, endurance, persecutions, sufferings—what kinds of things happened to me in Antioch, Iconium and Lystra, the persecutions I endured. Yet the Lord rescued me from all of them. In fact, everyone who wants to live a godly life in Christ Jesus will be persecuted, while evildoers and impostors will go from bad to worse, deceiving and being deceived. But as for you, continue in what you have learned and have become convinced of, because you know those from whom you learned it, and how from infancy you have known the Holy Scriptures, which are able to make you wise for salvation through faith in Christ Jesus. All Scripture is God-breathed and is useful for teaching, rebuking, correcting and training in righteousness, so that the servant of God may be thoroughly equipped for every good work.

In the presence of God and of Christ Jesus, who will judge the living and the dead, and in view of his appearing and his kingdom, I give you this charge: Preach the word; be prepared in season and out of season; correct, rebuke and encourage—with great patience and careful instruction. For the time will come when people will not put up with sound doctrine. Instead, to suit their own desires, they will gather around them a great number of teachers to say what their itching ears want to hear. They will turn their ears away from the truth and turn aside to myths. But you, keep your head in all situations, endure hardship, do the work of an evangelist, discharge all the duties of your ministry.

For I am already being poured out like a drink offering, and the time for my departure is near. I have fought the good fight, I have finished the race, I have kept the faith. Now there is in store for me the crown of righteousness, which the Lord, the righteous Judge, will award to me on that day—and not only to me, but also to all who have longed for his appearing.

Do your best to come to me quickly, for Demas, because he loved this world, has deserted me and has gone to Thessalonica. Crescens has gone to Galatia, and Titus to Dalmatia. Only Luke is with me. Get Mark and bring him with you, because he is helpful to me in my ministry. I sent Tychicus to Ephesus. When you come, bring the cloak that I left with Carpus at Troas, and my scrolls, especially the parchments.

Alexander the metalworker did me a great deal of harm. The Lord will repay him for what he has done. You too should be on your guard against him, because he strongly opposed our message.

At my first defense, no one came to my support, but everyone deserted me. May it not be held against them. But the Lord stood at my side and gave me strength, so that through me the message might be fully proclaimed and all the Gentiles might hear it. And I was delivered from the lion's mouth. The Lord will rescue me from every evil attack and will bring me safely to his heavenly kingdom. To him be glory for ever and ever. Amen.

Greet Priscilla and Aquila and the household of Onesiphorus. Erastus stayed in Corinth, and I left Trophimus sick in Miletus. Do your best to get here before winter. Eubulus greets you, and so do Pudens, Linus, Claudia and all the brothers and sisters.

The Lord be with your spirit. Grace be with you all.

Recommended: Listen to the podcast "Staying Faithful to God by Choice" at melanienewton.com/podcasts as an introduction to the whole study.

Staying Faithful to God by Choice

"The righteous will flourish like a palm tree, they will grow like a cedar of Lebanon; planted in the house of the Lord, they will flourish in the courts of our God. They will still bear fruit in old age, they will stay fresh and green, proclaiming, 'The Lord is upright; he is my Rock, and there is no wickedness in him.'" (Psalm 92:12-15)

WHAT DOES IT LOOK LIKE TO STAY FRESH AND GREEN?

- To stay fresh and green means to stay faithful to the Lord and useful to Him in bearing fruit.

- In many of his last letters, and especially in 2 Timothy, the Apostle Paul showed us in his life and in his words how we can stay faithful to Jesus for a lifetime.

ABOUT PAUL AND TIMOTHY

- Timothy was a teenager when he met Paul (Acts 16). Timothy's mom and grandmother were faithful Jewish women who taught the Old Testament scriptures to him. As the women heard Paul preach, they believed in Jesus, and so did Timothy.

- Paul invited Timothy to travel with him on his second missionary journey. Timothy helped Paul as he preached throughout Greece. When Paul was in Ephesus teaching the Ephesians about the amazing power of God, Timothy was there, too.

- When Paul was under Roman house arrest for two years, Timothy was right alongside him much of the time, unselfishly taking care of Paul's needs.

- After being set free, Paul and Timothy traveled to visit the churches they had founded. When they got to Ephesus, Paul left Timothy to teach truth to the church there while Paul went on to Macedonia. From there, he wrote the letter we have called *First Timothy*.

- Paul was arrested again and thrown into a cold dungeon in Rome. He wrote the letter called *Second Timothy*. In this letter, Paul reminds Timothy to stay faithful to the truth in spite of the persecution and suffering.

STAY FAITHFUL NO MATTER WHAT

"'Well done, good and faithful servant! You have been faithful with a few things; I will put you in charge of many things. Come and share your master's happiness!'" (Matthew 25:23)

- The definition of faithful is "unwavering in belief, consistently loyal." We all want those closest to us to remain faithful to us. Faithfulness is an important character quality.

- Our God is a faithful God. He is consistently loyal to those whom He loves and who place their trust in Him.

- God desires that we also be faithful to Him—to be unwavering in belief and consistently loyal to Him throughout our lifetime. The great news is that God is also the One who enables us to live faithfully as we choose to do so. We make the choice. He empowers us to live out that choice.

- Throughout this study of 2 Timothy, we will see faithfulness encouraged and lived out. We will see the importance of staying faithful to Jesus. We will see the importance of staying faithful to God's truth from His Word and what we learn from those who have taught us truth. *2 Timothy 1:12; 2 Timothy 3:14*

- We will see the importance of staying faithful to the community of believers, especially during tough times.

- Paul knew His God. He knew God was trustworthy. Paul chose to be unwavering in belief and consistently loyal to the Lord Jesus Christ—even as an old man in his 60s, in a Roman dungeon, with memories of persecution and beatings still engraved in his brain, and awaiting execution at any moment. He chose to stay fresh and green and write this beautiful letter of encouragement that not only fed Timothy's soul but millions of other Christians who have clung to its verses for the past 2000 years. We learn from Paul how to make choices to stay fresh and green while we are growing older.

MAKE CHOICES TO STAY FRESH AND GREEN WHILE GROWING OLD

- Choose to stay tuned to the needs of the people around you and desire to reach and teach them.

- Approach your Bible study with fresh eyes every day, looking for the new things the Lord will be teaching you and how you can share that with someone who needs to know it.

- Recognize God's work in your life every day, not just what He did years ago. That gives you a new song to share about what the Lord is doing in your life.

Through this study of 2 Timothy, we will learn how to stay faithful to our God—to be unwavering in belief and consistently loyal to Him as we live each day. We can stay faithful to His truth, to His people, to His ways, to His reputation, and to His purposes for our lives. And our faithful God is the One who enables us to do so. The wisdom of His Word and His Spirit living inside us together give us the ability to remain faithful, to stay fresh and green and fruitful for Him. The choice is up to you.

Let Jesus satisfy your heart with His faithfulness. Then, make the choice to stay faithful to Him for the rest of your life.

1: Truth and Faithfulness

DAY ONE STUDY

The ABCs of 2nd Timothy—Author, Background, and Context

Like any book you read, it always helps to know a bit about the author, the background setting for the story (i.e., past, present, future), and where the book fits into a series (that's the context). The same is true of Bible books.

AUTHOR

Paul identifies himself as the author of this letter written to Timothy. Paul, whose Hebrew name was Saul, was born in Tarsus, a major Roman city on the coast of southeast Asia Minor. Tarsus was the center for the tent making industry. Paul was trained in that craft as his occupation (his primary paying profession). As a Jewish Pharisee from the tribe of Benjamin, Paul was educated at the feet of Gamaliel, a well-respected rabbi of the day. Paul was an ardent persecutor of the early church until his life-changing conversion to Christianity

After believing in Jesus Christ as his Savior, Paul was sent by God as an apostle to take the gospel to the Gentiles. This was an amazing about-face for a committed Pharisee like Paul who ordinarily would have nothing to do with Gentiles. Paul wrote 13 letters that are included in the New Testament. Tradition has it that Paul was beheaded shortly after he wrote 2nd Timothy in 67 A.D. *(You can glean more about Paul's background from Acts 8:3; 9:1-31; 22:3-5; 26:9-11; and Galatians 1:11-24.)*

BACKGROUND

At the end of Paul's third missionary journey, he traveled to Jerusalem in the spring of 57 A.D. to deliver a collected offering from the Gentile churches to help the impoverished Jewish Christians. After being accused by the Jews of some technical violation of the Jewish Law, Paul was arrested by the Romans and spent the next two years in Caesarea as a prisoner (Acts 22-26). Paul appealed to Caesar so he was sent to Rome. There he lived under house arrest for another two years (Acts 27-28).

After Paul's release from this first Roman imprisonment (around 62 A.D.), he and Timothy traveled to Ephesus where Timothy was left to care for the house churches there. Paul wrote a letter (1st Timothy) around 64 A.D. to encourage Timothy in his work. Paul also went to Crete to establish churches and left Titus to oversee the work. He wrote a letter to Titus shortly thereafter. Some say Paul went to Spain, but we have no letters to confirm that. Around 67 A.D., Paul was again arrested during a time of great persecution that began three years earlier.

In 64 A.D., the Emperor Nero accused the Christians of burning Rome and began an all-out assault on them. Christians were mostly from the humbler walks of life, without prestige or influence, and many of them were slaves. The Roman historian Tacitus wrote that the Christians did not burn Rome. But somebody had to be made the scapegoat for it. Christians were targeted as "haters of mankind" because of their refusal to participate in Roman social life that was intertwined with pagan worship. In and around Rome, scores of Christians were arrested and put to death in the cruelest ways.

It was in the wake of this persecution that Paul was arrested in Asia Minor (western Turkey) and brought back to Rome. Whatever the crime was, his trial had proceeded far enough that he knew there was no hope of escape. In contrast to his first imprisonment when he lived in a rented house

(Acts 28:30), church tradition says that he was placed in the Mamertine Prison. Few prisons were as dim, dank, and dirty as the lower chamber Paul occupied. His friends even had a hard time finding out where he was being kept. Prisoners in the ancient world were rarely sent to prison as punishment. Rather, prisons typically served as holding cells for those awaiting trial or execution.

While waiting in the Roman dungeon for the "time of his departure," he wrote this last letter to Timothy, his "beloved son" and co-worker. Even in that dark hour, facing certain execution, Paul expresses no hint of regret for giving his life to the service of Christ and the Church. He was still confident that the Church would stay triumphant. And Paul knew that at his death he would go straight to the arms of His Lord Jesus Christ, whom he had loved and served so devotedly. *(Adapted from various resources)*

CONTEXT

Though 2nd Timothy is the last of Paul's letters in our New Testament, it is placed right after the book of 1st Timothy and before the letters to Titus and Philemon. This letter we know as 2nd Timothy is one of the most tender and moving of all of Paul's letters. It contains a lot of the same encouragement Paul gave in his first letter to Timothy plus an appeal for Timothy to get to Rome to be with him before winter.

1. What grabbed your attention from the ABCs above?

GET THE BIG PICTURE

Ask the Lord Jesus to teach you through His Word.

Paul's three letters—1st Timothy, 2nd Timothy and Titus—are called "pastoral epistles" because for the most part they are Paul's counsel to his assistants who served in the pastoral or shepherd-like function of the local churches in the regions of Ephesus and Crete.

The three letters address the issues facing local churches just like the one you are attending now—issues faced by the pastoral leaders as well as the members. Five major themes are woven throughout Paul's instruction to Timothy and Titus.

1) Teach and maintain truth and sound doctrine while guarding against error.

2) Identify leaders who will faithfully teach truth.

3) Guard the reputation of the church so that God may not be dishonored.

4) Do good deeds demonstrating the truth you believe.

5) Live dependently on Christ's power for all of the above.

These themes are especially evident in 1st Timothy and Titus, but you will see glimpses of them in 2nd Timothy as well.

Ready to get started? Let's go!

What does the Bible say? *(This is the "Observation" step in the process of Bible Study.)*

Where do we begin? Have you ever heard the saying, "You can't see the forest for the trees?" The best way to study any book of the Bible is to begin with the "forest" (survey the whole) and then proceed to the "trees" (the individual parts). We will start by getting an overview of what Paul wrote in his first letter to Timothy.

2. Paul wrote 1st Timothy just a short time before he wrote 2nd Timothy. In his second letter, Paul reminds Timothy of things he told him in the first letter. So read 1st Timothy chapters 1, 4, and 6 to get a feel for what he told his friend and ministry partner in that letter, especially related to Theme #1 mentioned above: *Teach and maintain truth and sound doctrine while guarding against error.* Make notes below.

Respond to the Lord about what He's shown you today.

Day Two Study

Today, you will get an overview of 2nd Timothy.

What does the Bible say? *(This is the "Observation" step in the process of Bible Study.)*

Ask the Lord Jesus to teach you through His Word.

3. Read 2nd Timothy. A copy of the letter is included in this study guide before Lesson One. You can mark repeated words and phrases as well as anything that grabs your attention. Pay attention to anything repeated from 1st Timothy. What did you notice?

What does it mean? *(This is the "Interpretation" step in the process of Bible Study.)*

Now, we will look at one theme in 2nd Timothy (common to Paul's pastoral letters): *Teach and maintain truth and sound doctrine while guarding against error.* This theme really breaks down into positive versus negative aspects. You will see both in 2nd Timothy. We'll look at the positive aspect today and the negative aspect tomorrow.

4. The **POSITIVE**: "teach and maintain truth and sound doctrine." Read the following verses. What does Paul emphasize in each?

    *   2 Timothy 1:8-10—

    *   2 Timothy 1:13-14—

    *   2 Timothy 2:2—

    *   2 Timothy 2:15—

    *   2 Timothy 3:14-15—

    *   2 Timothy 3:16-17—

    *   2 Timothy 4:2—

5. Once again, Paul emphasizes over and over a common message. In your own words, why is it necessary to teach and maintain truth and sound doctrine?

Respond to the Lord about what He's shown you today.

DAY THREE STUDY

Ask the Lord Jesus to teach you through His Word.

What does it mean? (This is the "Interpretation" step in the process of Bible Study.)

In the last section, you looked at the positive aspect of the theme, "teach and maintain truth and sound doctrine while guarding against error." In today's study, you will look at the negative part.

6. The **NEGATIVE**: "guard against error." Read the following verses to see what we are supposed to avoid when we encounter error and why.

• 2 Timothy 2:14 —

• 2 Timothy 2:16-18 —

• 2 Timothy 2:23 —

7. Read 2 Timothy 3:2-7 and 4:3-4. In general, where does error lead?

8. Once again, Paul emphasizes over and over a common message. In your own words, what is Paul teaching them to guard against…and why?

What application will you make to stay faithful to God? *(This is the "Application" step in the process of Bible Study.)*

9. If Paul made so many comments on the same subject (truth versus error), it should be taken seriously.

- What could happen to the local church…including you and me…if we do not seriously apply Paul's message to stay faithful to God's truth and guard against error?

- What specific actions can you or do you take in your daily life to ensure that you don't wander away from God's truth?

What does it mean to "Stay Faithful?"

Jesus told a parable to His disciples in Matthew 25. A man entrusts some treasure to his servants while he goes away. When he comes back, he evaluates how faithful the servants were with the treasure. The master's response to the two faithful servants is no doubt familiar to you,

> *"His master replied, 'Well done, good and faithful servant! You have been faithful with a few things; I will put you in charge of many things. Come and share your master's happiness!" (Matthew 25:23)*

The definition of faithful is "unwavering in belief, consistently loyal." We all want those closest to us—spouse, family members, friends, co-workers—to remain faithful to us. What security we feel when we know their loyalty is consistent and unwavering! Faithfulness is an important character quality.

Our God is a faithful God. He is consistently loyal to those whom He loves and who place their trust in Him. God desires that we also be faithful to Him—to be unwavering in belief and consistently loyal to Him—throughout our spiritual walk. And our God is the One Who protects and preserves that which He has entrusted to us—He enables us to live faithfully as we choose to do so. Faithfulness is a fruit of the Holy Spirit in us.

Focus on the Meaning: In this epistle, Paul emphasized the importance of faithfulness: God's faithfulness, Paul's faithfulness, Timothy's need to remain faithful, and the faithfulness or unfaithfulness of Paul's fellow workers and other servants of Christ. Paul was counting on God being faithful and providing what He had promised, namely, eternal life in Christ. (*Dr. Constable's Notes on 2 Timothy 2017 Edition,* p. 7)

Through this study of 2nd Timothy, you will learn how to make the choice to live faithfully to God every day for the rest of your life. And He will help you to do that.

Respond to the Lord about what He's shown you today.

Recommended: Listen to "Staying Faithful to God's Truth" at melanienewton.com/podcasts after doing this lesson to reinforce what you have learned. Use the listener guide on the next page.

Staying Faithful to God's Truth

TEACH AND MAINTAIN TRUTH; GUARD AGAINST ERROR.

- Any opinion or belief that contradicts established biblical truth can cause an infection in the Body of Christ. A spiritual infection is usually fed by looking to the wrong places to get your heart needs satisfied. The results are disappointment, fear, resentment, and many other negative thoughts and behaviors. Or it can be fed by a poor understanding of biblical truth. Women who never recognize and grasp biblical truth will be taken captive by whatever flashy teachings that come along and live unsatisfied, unstable lives. We see this in our world today.

- The answer to all spiritual infections is the truth that has been given to us in the Bible, especially in the New Testament. The writings of the New Testament are the work of the Holy Spirit revealing himself to the apostles and other disciples of Jesus. The historical reliability of the Scriptures is an important issue, and they (the Scriptures) can be investigated to show that the biblical records are trustworthy.

- Grasping truth has three parts: First, you dwell in the truth of God you can know. Next, you humbly accept what you don't know or understand. And then, you discern any teaching that you read or hear through the complete revelation of God's Word.

DWELL IN TRUTH YOU CAN KNOW.

- To dwell in truth is to make your home there. That means God's truth dominates your thoughts and attitudes, governs your life, and satisfies your heart.

- God gives us plenty of truth in the Bible that we can know and trust. 66 books, 1189 chapters!

- God wants us to know the truth He has revealed to us, to make our home in that truth. *Ephesians 1:17-19*

HUMBLY ACCEPT WHAT YOU DON'T KNOW OR UNDERSTAND.

- Some things we read in the Bible we don't understand now but might in the future. There is much we can know now. But there are things we'll never know or understand. *Deuteronomy 29:29*

- We can do our best to try to understand what is written. When you run across something that you can't seem to understand from a Bible passage, make the choice to humbly accept what you don't know or understand.

DISCERN ALL TEACHING THROUGH THE COMPLETE REVELATION OF GOD'S WORD.

1. Evaluate what you read and hear by comparing it with the whole Bible.

- Read any verse in the context of the passage where it is found—the paragraph, the chapter, and the book.

- Examine the original words to see what the writer meant and what the audience likely understood.

- Look at other verses with similar content to let the Bible interpret itself. And you should always ask the Holy Spirit for understanding.

2. Avoid the "look-imagine-see dragon" when viewing any verse.

The "look-imagine-see" dragon shows up this way: someone *looks* at a verse or passage, *imagines* what they want it to say, then in their mind *sees* what they have imagined through twisting word meanings and interpretations. Once it starts, it's like a fiery dragon burning truth in its path. Cultural influence on Bible study feeds this dragon.

- Tame the "look-imagine-see dragon" by considering the Bible as sufficient on its own, not needing to be "improved."

- Tame the "look-imagine-see dragon" by basing your faith on what **is** in God's Word, not something you've just heard about it and not something you're imagining to be there.

- Tame the "look-imagine-see dragon" by following the inductive process for Bible Study—observation, interpretation, and application. Then, you can dwell in truth you can know.

The way to stay faithful to God's truth and guard against error is to dwell in truth you can know, humbly accept what you don't know or understand, and discern all teaching through the complete revelation of God's Word.

We'll never know all there is to know about God. There will always be some mystery about Him. But there's plenty enough revealed in the Bible to satisfy your desire to **know him truthfully** and to know how to live your life in Christ truthfully.

Let Jesus satisfy your heart with His faithfulness. Then, make the choice to stay faithful to Him for the rest of your life.

2: Stay Faithful without Fear

2 Timothy 1:1-7

DAY ONE STUDY—GET THE BIG PICTURE

What does the Bible say?

Let's start digging into this wonderful letter from God to us. For every lesson, we will begin with reading the whole passage to get the big picture before we study the verses more closely. Sometimes, we will include verses from the previous lesson to show continuity.

Ask the Lord Jesus to teach you through His Word.

Read the Bible passage below (NIV). Use your own method (colored pencils, lines, shapes) to mark 1) anything that grabs your attention, 2) words you want to understand, and 3) anything repeated in this passage. Draw arrows between thoughts that connect. Put a star ✱ next to anything you think relates to being faithful or staying faithful.

1 Paul, an apostle of Christ Jesus by the will of God, in keeping with the promise of life that is in Christ Jesus,

2 To Timothy, my dear son: Grace, mercy and peace from God the Father and Christ Jesus our Lord.

3 I thank God, whom I serve, as my ancestors did, with a clear conscience, as night and day I constantly remember you in my prayers. 4 Recalling your tears, I long to see you, so that I may be filled with joy. 5 I am reminded of your sincere faith, which first lived in your grandmother Lois and in your mother Eunice and, I am persuaded, now lives in you also.

6 For this reason I remind you to fan into flame the gift of God, which is in you through the laying on of my hands. 7 For the Spirit God gave us does not make us timid, but gives us power, love and self-discipline.

1. What grabbed your attention from these verses?

2. What verses or specific words do you want to understand better?

3. What topics are repeated in this passage or continue an earlier discussion in this letter?

4. What verses illustrate or help you understand what staying faithful looks like?

5. From this lesson's passage, choose one verse to dwell upon all week long. Write it in the space below. Ask God to teach you through this verse.

Respond to the Lord about what He's shown you today.

DAY TWO STUDY

Read 2 Timothy 1:1-7.

Ask the Lord Jesus to teach you through His Word.

Historical Insight: Who is Timothy? Timothy was born and reared in Lystra (central Turkey). His mother, Eunice, and grandmother, Lois, were devout Jews who became believers in Christ. Timothy's father was a Greek. There is no mention of him beyond that. Timothy first heard Paul preach the gospel on Paul's first visit to Lystra and trusted in Christ then. In essence, Paul was Timothy's spiritual father. When Paul came back to Lystra, Timothy joined Paul on the rest of his 2nd missionary journey.

During that time, Timothy helped to establish churches at Philippi, Thessalonica, and Berea. When Paul left Berea to go to Athens, Timothy and Silas stayed behind before later joining Paul in Corinth. Timothy was sent to Thessalonica to strengthen the faith of believers there. He also traveled with Paul to minister to churches in both Greece and Asia (western Turkey).

Six of Paul's epistles to churches include Timothy in the salutations meaning Timothy was with him when Paul wrote the letters. Acts does not tell us whether Timothy was with Paul during Paul's two-year imprisonment at Caesarea. But he was with Paul during his house arrest in Rome. After Paul's release (around 62 A.D.), Timothy and Paul traveled to Ephesus where Timothy was left to care for the church. Paul wrote 1st Timothy around 64 A.D. from Macedonia.

Paul wrote 2nd Timothy (~ 67 A.D.) while Timothy was still in Ephesus. The area surrounding Ephesus probably had a number of young churches, not just one, with each church led by elders. Timothy was sent as an "apostolic representative," that is, as Paul's substitute. He had the authority to oversee worship and appoint elders and deacons as well as maintain the teaching of truth and sound Christian doctrine.

According to *Foxe's Book of Martyrs,* written several centuries later (1563), Timothy remained in Ephesus until 97 A.D. During a pagan celebration of a feast called "Catagogion," Timothy severely reproved the people in the procession for their ridiculous idolatry. This antagonized the partygoers who beat him with clubs "in so dreadful a manner that he expired of the bruises two days later." *(The above information is gathered from Acts 16-20, most of Paul's letters, and Foxe's Book of Martyrs)*

What does it mean?

6. After identifying himself as Paul, an apostle of Christ Jesus by the will of God (a declaration common to all his letters), what does he say next in v. 1? Why would this be an important truth to him at this time?

7. Looking at vv. 2-7, what words and phrases reveal the depth of Paul's relationship with Timothy?

8. Based on what you read in the "Historical Insight" above, why is their relationship so meaningful to Paul?

9. In 2 Timothy 1:3, Paul says he serves God with a clear conscience as his forefathers did. Read Hebrews 11:17-40. What sort of spiritual heritage did Paul's Jewish forefathers leave him?

> **Focus on the Meaning:** To have a good, or pure, conscience does not mean that we have never sinned or do not commit acts of sin. Rather, it means that the underlying direction and motive of life is to obey and please God, so that acts of sin are habitually recognized as such and faced before God. (*Dr. Constable's Notes on 2 Timothy 2017 Edition*, p. 8)

10. According to 2 Timothy 1:5, who were Timothy's primary spiritual mentors as he was growing up? What gift did they impart to him? See also 2 Timothy 3:14-15.

> **Historical Insight:** Timothy's mother Eunice was Jewish, but her own father was apparently not very orthodox. He violated one of the clear commands of the Law in arranging a match for his daughter with a Gentile (Acts 16:1). Later, when Timothy was born, he wasn't circumcised (16:3). So it seems that neither Eunice's father nor husband were observant of Judaism. But Eunice was. Paul praised her for her "genuine faith," which she shared in common with her own mother Lois. Eunice imparted that faith to her son, Timothy, and...equipped him for a lifetime of usefulness for God. Eunice is an encouragement for every woman faced with the daunting task of nurturing the spiritual life of her children. (*The Word in Life Study Bible*, p. 746)

What application will you make to stay faithful to God?

11. Consider the role of mentoring / discipling in your life.

- Have you had a spiritual parent or mentor like Paul? If so, who, and how did that person influence you to love and serve Christ?

- Have you had influence on a younger Christian like Timothy? If so, who, and what did you do to influence him/her to love and serve Christ?

- If you have influence over children (parent, grandparent, teacher, friend, or other), what are you doing to impart a spiritual legacy, or heritage, to them?

Respond to the Lord about what He's shown you today.

DAY THREE STUDY

Read 2 Timothy 1:1-7.

Ask the Lord Jesus to teach you through His Word.

What does it mean?

12. According to 2 Timothy 1:5, we know that Timothy possessed sincere faith, which is a precious treasure especially in a church leader. He also had been given a spiritual gift for leadership and teaching.

- What is said about this gift in 1 Timothy 1:18; 4:14?

- Because of this faith, what was Paul encouraging Timothy to do with his God-given gift?

    From the Greek: The Greek word translated as "fan into flame" or "kindle afresh" means to "kindle up, inflame one's mind." The word picture is that of a pair of bellows used on burning embers to invigorate a flame.

- What would it look like to "fan into flame" or "kindle up" a spiritual gift?

- What would the opposite look like?

13. Read 1 Corinthians 16:10 and 1 Timothy 4:12. The implication in these verses is that Timothy had a tendency to be timid or be afraid when facing challenges.

> **Focus on the Meaning:** Fear is a normal human emotion designed by God to alert us to danger so that we will take action against it. The right response is to act on it by either fleeing from the danger or facing it head on. God gave humans the gift of fear as an emotion before sin (Genesis 2:16-17) to lead us to obey Him. A wrong response would be to do nothing or to let fear controls you so that you become its slave.

- According to 2 Timothy 1:7, what does not come from God?

- To respond rightly to fear, what does God's Spirit provide to us? See also Romans 8:15.

> **From the Greek:** Let's define those words. "Power" comes from *dynamis*, meaning "the power of God to make you strong and able." It is God's power manifested in us. "Love" is *agape*, meaning unconditional love, God's kind of love. "Self-control" comes from *sophronismos*, meaning "soundness of mind, moderation, self-control, disciplined mind." It is the opposite of hysteria.

14. Why are these three qualities so important for those who want to serve Christ with their lives?

15. If God's spirit within us is one of power, love, and discipline, what should (or could) characterize our response towards life's hardships? Glean the following verses for your answer:

- 2 Corinthians 12:9-10 —

- Philippians 4:12-13, 19 —

- Hebrews 4:15-16 —

Think About It: "Craving, cringing, panicky fear is one of the devil's greatest weapons. I have a better chance of solving problems if I deal with them in a spirit of power, love, and a sound mind. (Tim Stevenson, *Mind Games*)

What application will you make to stay faithful to God?

16. About "fanning into flame" your spiritual gifts:

> In the RESOURCES section, find a list of spiritual gifts with descriptions of each and a link to an online assessment that will help you to discover your gifts. Most of the spiritual gifts are described in Romans 12:3-8, 1 Corinthians 12:4-30 and Ephesians 4:11.

- Do you recognize the spiritual gift(s) God has given you?

- How are you using your gift(s) and experience for serving Christ?

17. Timothy may have had a tendency to be timid and fearful when faced with a challenge. What specific fears or inabilities tend to get in the way of your service to Christ? How can you apply 2 Timothy 1:7 to your life?

Respond to the Lord about what He's shown you today.

> **Recommended:** Listen to "Staying Faithful without Fear" at melanienewton.com/podcasts after doing this lesson to reinforce what you have learned. Use the listener guide on the next page.

Staying Faithful without Fear

WHAT FAITH IS AND IS NOT

- Faith is not a blind belief or mindless gullibility. Faith is not a life of passivity and doing nothing. Faith is not a religious feeling from performing some ritual.

- The word "faith" means a "belief, trust, and commitment of mind and heart to something or someone."
  - ✓ Faith is **intelligent**. That means first you need to know about the something or someone. It is based on information about the object of your faith.
  - ✓ Faith is **decisive**. It involves the element of assent or agreement that the information about that someone or something is true.
  - ✓ Faith **requires an act of the will**. Any conscious choice that involves trust, reliance, or dependence on someone or something requires a deliberate action to choose to trust the information. It is the difference between walking alongside a pool of water (seeing it is there) and jumping into the water (experiencing the water personally).

- Simply put, faith is a full commitment to Christ. Instead of believing in your own ability to earn God's favor, you now trust in what Christ has done for you. That's biblical faith.

- By God's grace, you are saved through your faith (Ephesians 2:8-9). It is by your faith alone that you are saved. It is the gift of God—not by works, so that no one can boast of their efforts. Your response is to be one of faith.

- Trust or faith is always an issue of credibility. It is hard to trust God if you don't know Him. The more you know Him, the easier it is to trust Him. Knowing God's character plus His promises gives you plenty of reasons to consider Him trustworthy.

  God's plan for your life is simple. Follow His Son. But you won't follow someone you don't trust. You can't trust someone you don't know, and you cannot know Christ apart from His Word. (Rebecca Carrell, heartstrongfaith.com)

FEAR CAN KEEP YOU FROM STAYING FAITHFUL TO GOD'S PURPOSES FOR YOU.

- The Greek word translated as "fan into flame" literally means to "kindle up, inflame one's mind." The word picture is that of blowing on burning embers to invigorate a flame.

- Fear might keep you from using and growing your spiritual gifts, from staying faithful to God's purposes for you.

  "For the Spirit God gave us does not make us timid, but gives us power, love and self-discipline." (2 Timothy 1:7)

FEAR IS A GIFT FROM GOD.

- Fear is a normal human emotion designed by God to alert us to danger so that we will take action against it. We are supposed to act on it by either fleeing from the danger or facing it head on. Fear as an emotion is a gift from God.

- Fear has a dark side as well. When we look at life just with our own eyes, we become fearful, pessimistic, & negative. We think to ourselves, "Nothing's going to work. I don't know if I can get through this." But when we look at the Bible and see how God helped everyday people like you and I, the Holy Spirit takes the Word of God to strengthen us and give us courage that we didn't know we had.

- The Bible teaches that we can face life's realities, face any fearful situation, with courage and peace by entrusting ourselves and our loved ones to a God who loves us dearly.

A PROCESS TO APPLY FAITH TO ANY FEAR

1. **Confront it:** What fears do you have right now? Think about them. The worst ones, the real ones, and the imaginary ones.

2. **Ask about each one:** What is my worst-case scenario? Consider just one of those fears. What is the worst that could happen? Think realistically.

3. **Consider this:** If the worst I can imagine happens, could I handle it through the presence and power of Jesus Christ? As a believer, you have the power of the One who created the universe living inside of you. Can He help you get through anything? Yes!

4. **Remember** these four truths and speak them to yourself:
   - ✓ God loves you. John 16:27; Romans 5:5, Ephesians 5:1
   - ✓ God knows what is going on in your life. Matthew 6:31-32; Psalm 139:1-10
   - ✓ God can do something about it. Genesis 18:14; Luke 1:37; Mark 10:27
   - ✓ You can trust His goodness in whatever He chooses to do. Psalm 119:68; Proverbs 3:5
5. **Pray:** Prayer is simply talking to God about anything and everything. Thank the Lord for His presence and His goodness. Ask Him for the courage and peace to ride out the storm.

6. **Live life securely in Him:** Take common sense precautions. Be wise in the world. Trust God to show you what to do and to give you strength when you are weak.

> Where there is faith, there is a voice calling, keep walking. You're not alone in this world. Where there is faith, there is a peace like a child sleeping, hope everlasting in He who is able to bear every burden, to heal every hurt in your heart. It is a wonderful, powerful place where there is faith. ("Where There Is Faith," from the album *Simply 4Him*)

Let Jesus satisfy your heart with His faithfulness. Then, make the choice to stay faithful to Him for the rest of your life.

3: Faithfulness without Shame

2 Timothy 1:7-18

DAY ONE STUDY—GET THE BIG PICTURE

What does the Bible say?

Ask the Lord Jesus to teach you through His Word.

Read the Bible passage below (NIV, including verses from the last lesson). Use your own method (colored pencils, lines, shapes) to mark 1) anything that grabs your attention, 2) words you want to understand, and 3) anything repeated in this passage or from a previous part of the letter. Draw arrows between thoughts that connect. Put a star ✱ next to anything you think relates to being faithful.

1 *6 For this reason I remind you to fan into flame the gift of God, which is in you through the laying on of my hands. 7 For the Spirit God gave us does not make us timid, but gives us power, love and self-discipline. 8 So do not be ashamed of the testimony about our Lord or of me his prisoner. Rather, join with me in suffering for the gospel, by the power of God. 9 He has saved us and called us to a holy life—not because of anything we have done but because of his own purpose and grace. This grace was given us in Christ Jesus before the beginning of time, 10 but it has now been revealed through the appearing of our Savior, Christ Jesus, who has destroyed death and has brought life and immortality to light through the gospel. 11 And of this gospel I was appointed a herald and an apostle and a teacher. 12 That is why I am suffering as I am. Yet this is no cause for shame, because I know whom I have believed, and am convinced that he is able to guard what I have entrusted to him until that day.*

13 What you heard from me, keep as the pattern of sound teaching, with faith and love in Christ Jesus. 14 Guard the good deposit that was entrusted to you—guard it with the help of the Holy Spirit who lives in us. 15 You know that everyone in the province of Asia has deserted me, including Phygelus and Hermogenes.

16 May the Lord show mercy to the household of Onesiphorus, because he often refreshed me and was not ashamed of my chains. 17 On the contrary, when he was in Rome, he searched hard for me until he found me. 18 May the Lord grant that he will find mercy from the Lord on that day! You know very well in how many ways he helped me in Ephesus.

1. What grabbed your attention from these verses?

2. What verses or specific words do you want to understand better?

3. What topics are repeated in this passage or continue an earlier discussion in this letter?

4. What verses illustrate or help you understand what staying faithful looks like?

5. From this lesson's passage, choose one verse to dwell upon all week long. Write it in the space below. Ask God to teach you through this verse.

Respond to the Lord about what He's shown you today.

DAY TWO STUDY

Read 2 Timothy 1:7-18.

Ask the Lord Jesus to teach you through His Word.

What does it mean?

> **Historical Insight:** One of the most difficult things for ancient history students to get their heads around when first exploring the subject is the place Mediterranean societies gave to honor and shame. Honor was universally regarded as the ultimate asset for human beings, and shame the ultimate deficit—so much so that academics frequently refer to Egyptian, Greek, and Roman societies simply as "honor-shame" cultures. Much of life revolved around ensuring you and your family received public honor and avoided public shame...humility was rarely, if ever, considered virtuous. (John Dickson, *Humilitas: A Lost Key to Life, Love and Leadership,* pp. 83-95)

6. What is the earnest counsel Paul gives Timothy in verse 8?

Focus on the Meaning: Three times in this chapter Paul uses the word "ashamed." Shame is a feeling arising from something that has been done, not necessarily by oneself but by a hated cause such as Christianity or someone with whom one associates who has been discredited (Paul). The Greek word translated "ashamed" does not imply that Timothy was ashamed, but it is rather an admonition to not start being ashamed.

7. According to Paul, he is the prisoner of whom (v. 8)? See also Ephesians 3:1; 4:1; Philemon 1, 9.

8. What pressures might pull at Timothy to be ashamed to speak openly about the Lord or Paul?

Historical Insight: After the burning of Rome in 64 A.D., the Roman Christians were accused of "hatred against mankind." This perception likely began in their refusal to participate in Rome's social and civic life, which was intertwined with pagan worship. That despicable label for Christians (hating humanity) would have spread throughout the Empire. Paul had been considered a "ringleader" of these people (Acts 24:5). (Derrick G. Jeter, *Historical Background of Paul's Final Imprisonment,* posted August 14, 2017 on insightforliving.org)

9. According to 2 Timothy 1:12 and Romans 1:16, what kept Paul from being ashamed of himself?

10. In 2 Timothy 1:8-10, Paul describes the gospel message he has received from God and entrusted to Timothy. Timothy was not to be ashamed of this gospel and was to take his share of suffering for it. What key words and phrases does Paul use to describe the gospel?

Scriptural Insight: God's plan to save lost sinners was made in eternity past (Ephesians 1:4; 1 Peter 1:20; Revelation 13:8). (*NIV Study Bible 1985 Edition,* note on 1:9, p. 1844)

11. In verse 11, Paul defines himself in 3 specific roles. God appointed Paul to be a preacher or herald (*kerux*, "one who announces and proclaims"), an apostle (*apostolos*, "one who is sent"), and a teacher (*didaskalos*, "one who imparts knowledge and gives instruction"). How are these roles the cause of his suffering (verse 12)?

Think About It: An "apostle" today is anyone who is sent by God to a location or people. That could be your town and neighbors or a foreign village. Once sent, your job is to be a herald there proclaiming the good news about Jesus and then teach those who respond. Where have you been sent as a herald or teacher?

12. What motivated Paul to endure suffering as awful as imprisonment (v.12)?

Dependent Living: Paul's choice of words in the first half can be understood this way: "I know Him in whom I have trusted and still am trusting, and I became convinced and still am convinced that He is able to guard…" Ongoing trust and conviction no matter what! What is being guarded by Christ? At the end of verse 12, some translations say "what I have entrusted **to Him,**" likely referring to Paul's confidence in his "promise of life (v. 1)" that is in Christ Jesus. Like putting money in a bank that you trust, you (like Paul) can depend on God to fulfill His promise of eternal life to you as you have committed your very self to Him. Jesus made this promise of security in John 10:27-28. Others say "what has been entrusted **to me,**" likely referring to the gospel message of which Paul was appointed a herald and an apostle. The gospel is something valuable that God entrusted to Paul to preach and is being entrusted to Timothy to do likewise. So both translations are equally true.

13. Focusing on vv. 13-14:

- What "treasure" is Timothy supposed to guard? See also 1 Timothy 1:11; 6:20; and Titus 1:3.

- What would it look like to protect this treasure against loss?

- How is he able to guard this treasure?

Dependent Living: We are responsible to adhere to and teach sound doctrine as well as live a godly life based on that sound doctrine. We can do this through the indwelling Holy Spirit. This is a cooperative effort. The Holy Spirit is the third person of the Trinity. He is given to every believer at the moment of salvation (Romans 8:9; 1 Corinthians 12:13). He is directly involved in both aspects of guarding the deposit of the gospel, namely, holding to sound doctrine (John 14:26) and living a godly life (Galatians 5:16-21). If you know the truth and are guarding it, you won't be ashamed.

What application will you make to stay faithful to God?

14. Being ashamed of the gospel:

- When might someone tend to be ashamed to speak up about Christ or the gospel?

- How can you practice the truth of 2 Timothy 1:7 to help you tell others the good news about Jesus and to guard against being ashamed of it?

Respond to the Lord about what He's shown you today.

DAY THREE STUDY

Read 2 Timothy 1:8-18.

Ask the Lord Jesus to teach you through His Word.

15. In vv. 15-18, Paul uses exaggeration to describe how his friends from the province of Asia reacted to his imprisonment. What does he say about them?

Focus on the Meaning: "Deserted" means "to turn away from." Just because they turned away from Paul doesn't mean they turned away from the gospel. Yet, being abandoned by those who were once his colleagues caused Paul more suffering.

16. How did Onesiphorus respond differently? Be specific as you list all that is said about him.

17. Define the word "refreshed."

18. Paul referred to this ministry of being refreshed in his other letters. What do you learn about this in the following verses? Who was refreshed and how (if given)?

- 1 Corinthians 16:17-18—

- 2 Corinthians 7:13-14—

- Philemon 1:7, 20-21—

19. Back to 2 Timothy 1:16-18. Why would being refreshed by Onesiphorus have been important to Paul at this time?

> **Historical Insight:** The Mamertine Prison (where Paul likely was kept at this time) could have been called the "House of Darkness." Few prisons were as dim, dank, and dirty as the lower chamber Paul occupied. Known in earlier times as the Tullianum dungeon, its "neglect, darkness, and stench" gave it "a hideous and terrifying appearance," according to Roman historian Sallust. (Derrick G. Jeter, *Historical Background of Paul's Final Imprisonment,* posted August 14, 2017 on insightforliving.org)

20. What self-sacrifices did Onesiphorus make in order to refresh Paul in Rome?

What application will you make to stay faithful to God?

21. About endurance and the need for refreshing:

- Think of a time in your life that tested your physical or emotional endurance. What kept you going? Did someone refresh you?

- How did you help someone else endure a physically or emotionally trying time? How did you refresh them?

22. Choose one missionary (someone you know or someone your church supports) and pray this week that the grace of God will sustain them.

Respond to the Lord about what He's shown you today.

> **Recommended:** Listen to "Staying Faithful to Our Treasure in Jesus Christ" at melanienewton.com/podcasts after doing this lesson to reinforce what you have learned. Use the listener guide on the next page.

Staying Faithful to Our Treasure in Jesus Christ

GUARD THE TREASURE.

"Guard the good deposit that was entrusted to you—guard it with the help of the Holy Spirit who lives in us." (2 Timothy 1:14, NIV)

- The Greek word translated "good deposit" means something that is beautiful, precious, magnificent. The NAS translation uses the word "treasure." Guard the treasure.

- From the context, we can see that the treasure is the sound teaching of the gospel wrapped up in Jesus Christ. The truth about Jesus is treasure. Guard that treasure.

THE EPHESIAN TREASURE CHEST

- Two words described Ephesus—prominent and obsessed. It was a prominent place because of its location and population. It was obsessed as a center for spiritualism in the Roman world filled with magic, psychics, astrologers, and palm readers. The people had a huge fear of evil powers that could make their life miserable. Anything they could count on to defeat the enemy so they could live a "successful" life was worth a try.

- For the Ephesians, life was all about who had power. And their identity came from their power sources. That was reflected in their treasure chests. They found out that their own treasure chest was worthless compared to what Paul offered them.

GOD'S TREASURE CHEST IS JESUS CHRIST.

- Paul spent 3 years in Ephesus, teaching daily. While there, God did extraordinary miracles through Paul (Acts 19:11-12). The Greek word used means "to hit the mark like one who is throwing a javelin or arrow." God was targeting their need. God demonstrated to those superstitious, obsessed people that He was more powerful than their magicians and other religious substitutes. He knew what they really needed—Himself!

- Because God targeted the Ephesians' need, many followed Jesus and became disciple-makers as they went to their towns and planted churches all over western Turkey, multiplying Paul's ministry. Ephesus stayed prominent—with a new identity as one of the leading centers of Christianity for hundreds of years. And many Ephesians became obsessed with a new purpose and object of worship—Jesus.

- God does that for us, too. He gives us a new identity in Christ and a new purpose as we follow Jesus and live for Him daily. And when we trust in His power in our lives to meet our needs, we recognize that the treasure we have in Jesus Christ is greater than anything we can substitute for Him.

THE MODERN TREASURE CHEST

- Our culture in this age of reason is drawn to supernatural power though not necessarily God's power.

- Westerners are interested in the supernatural because we seek anything that will satisfy the spiritual hunger in our soul and "guarantee" successful living.

- The treasure we already have in Jesus Christ is more valuable than any of those substitutes. The problem is that we have to recognize that substitute treasure is worthless.

SUBSTITUTE TREASURE IS WORTHLESS.

- When Christians lose confidence in the one true God to meet our needs, we begin to rely on the aid of other "powers" such as mystical experiences, formulas for "success," and lucky practices. When we are no longer convinced that the treasure we have in Jesus Christ is effective to meet our need, we often look to substitutes, even subconsciously.

- When we recognize those substitutes, we should get rid of them and cling to our treasure in Christ alone.

JESUS CHRIST IS MORE POWERFUL THAN ANY SUBSTITUTE.

- Paul told Timothy that Jesus is his power to get through anything. We have an incredible power source. In fact, the Greek word for power, *dunamis*, is where we get our word dynamite and is often translated as "miracles" in the New Testament. *2 Timothy 1:8-10*

- Our identity comes from our power source, that which we rely upon. The power of God is available to every believer to meet every need. His dynamite power is **for** us and **within** us. *Ephesians 1:19-22*

- We can picture ourselves sitting with Jesus in the heavenly realms, with our treasure chest—all that we receive in Him. We can rest in that and all the treasure that comes with it. That's the way to guarantee successful living—God's way of successful living.

- The treasure you have in Jesus Christ is more powerful and valuable than anything you could substitute for Him.

YOUR TREASURE CHEST

Are you willing to get rid of your substitutes and cling to your treasure in Christ alone? Jesus Christ is your treasure. You can say with your heart to Him, "My treasure in you, Lord Jesus, is more powerful and valuable than anything I could substitute for You. Please confirm that in my heart."

Let Jesus satisfy your heart with His faithfulness. Then, make the choice to stay faithful to Him for the rest of your life.

4: The Hard Work of Faithfulness

2 Timothy 2:1-13

DAY ONE STUDY—GET THE BIG PICTURE

What does the Bible say?

Ask the Lord Jesus to teach you through His Word.

Read the Bible passage below (NIV, including verses from the last lesson). Use any method to mark 1) anything that grabs your attention, 2) words you want to understand, and 3) anything repeated in this passage or from a previous part of the letter. Draw arrows between thoughts that connect. Put a star ✱ next to anything you think relates to being faithful.

1 *13 What you heard from me, keep as the pattern of sound teaching, with faith and love in Christ Jesus. 14 Guard the good deposit that was entrusted to you—guard it with the help of the Holy Spirit who lives in us.*

2 *You then, my son, be strong in the grace that is in Christ Jesus. 2 And the things you have heard me say in the presence of many witnesses entrust to reliable people who will also be qualified to teach others. 3 Join with me in suffering, like a good soldier of Christ Jesus. 4 No one serving as a soldier gets entangled in civilian affairs, but rather tries to please his commanding officer. 5 Similarly, anyone who competes as an athlete does not receive the victor's crown except by competing according to the rules. 6 The hardworking farmer should be the first to receive a share of the crops. 7 Reflect on what I am saying, for the Lord will give you insight into all this.*

8 Remember Jesus Christ, raised from the dead, descended from David. This is my gospel, 9 for which I am suffering even to the point of being chained like a criminal. But God's word is not chained. 10 Therefore I endure everything for the sake of the elect, that they too may obtain the salvation that is in Christ Jesus, with eternal glory.

11 Here is a trustworthy saying:
If we died with him, we will also live with him;
12 if we endure, we will also reign with him. If we [deny] him, he will also [deny] us;
13 if we are faithless, he remains faithful, for he cannot [deny] himself.

> **From the Greek:** All other translations use "deny" in verses 12-13, so I have substituted that for "disown" (NIV). No one can 'own' Christ anyway.

1. What grabbed your attention from these verses?

2. What verses or specific words do you want to understand better?

3. What topics are repeated in this passage or continue an earlier discussion in this letter?

4. What verses illustrate or help you understand what staying faithful looks like?

5. From this lesson's passage, choose one verse to dwell upon all week long. Write it in the space below. Ask God to teach you through this verse.

Respond to the Lord about what He's shown you today.

DAY TWO STUDY

Read 2 Timothy 2:1-13.

Ask the Lord Jesus to teach you through His Word.

What does it mean?

As a result of Paul's missionary journeys and the spread of the gospel of Jesus Christ, local churches were formed. These believers met in homes or wherever they could gather to continue in the apostles' teachings and to live out the Christian faith among one another as well as among the unbelieving world.

When Paul visited Ephesus after his release from Roman house arrest (Acts 28:31), he discovered that the church had been plagued with all kinds of spiritual problems during his absence. The city itself, with all of its corruption and idolatry, was a spiritual battleground for the congregation of believers.

Having faithfully done all he could to develop and teach the truths of the gospel throughout his ministry, Paul is concerned near the end of his life that his faithful disciples would entrust these truths to other faithful Christians who would in turn entrust them to others. Paul viewed this body of sound Christian doctrine as a special stewardship from God that must be managed with great care. Since this truth leads to godliness by pointing believers to Jesus Christ, it was the most valuable of treasures. The local church leaders were not only to faithfully teach truth to their congregations but also to sternly resist all attempts to undermine, pollute, or attack the true gospel.

6. In 2 Timothy 2:1, what is Paul urging his spiritual son Timothy to do?

7. Why would Paul tell Timothy to be strong in "grace" rather than something like "knowledge?" See also 2 Timothy 1:7-9 and 4:17.

Dependent Living: The Greek word translated "be strong" in 2:1 indicates the need for continual dependence on God. The believer is empowered for strength by God. It is a gift included in God's grace.

8. How did Timothy learn about God's gospel of grace (v. 2)?

Focus on the Meaning: Many heard the exact same teaching from Paul. Timothy heard it over and over as he traveled with Paul for many years.

9. Paul uses the word "entrust" several times in this letter. Review 1:12-14.

To whom is Timothy supposed to entrust the gospel and for what purpose (v. 2)? Note: Some older translations say "men," but the Greek word used refers to people, both men and women.

Think About It: The [Christian] teacher is a link in the living chain which stretches unbroken from this present moment back to Jesus Christ. The glory of teaching is that it links the present with the earthly life of Jesus Christ. (*Constable's Notes on 2 Timothy 2017 Edition,* p. 17)

10. Why would faithfulness (or reliability) be more important than position or influence?

11. As Timothy preached and taught, he would face suffering, but he should also be able to stay faithful and endure. In verses 3-6, Paul uses 3 vivid examples to motivate his beloved son Timothy, illustrating the attitude that Christ's followers must have to stay faithful through suffering. What are the three examples?

12. Let's examine Paul's illustration of a good soldier.

  • What are the characteristics of a good soldier on active duty (vv. 3-4)?

  • In what ways does a believer "endure" or "suffer" hardship in the same manner as a soldier on active duty?

Historical Insight: Roman soldiers would not be distracted by "civilian" concerns: entertainment, politics, weather, or other non-military matters that do not relate to their specific mission. They had a job to do. Instead, their focus was on fulfilling the orders of their commander. In this word picture, Christ is the one who has enlisted Timothy. His goal was the mission for which God had called him.

13. Paul stressed the importance of remaining free from entanglement with "civilian affairs" (pursuits of life) as a soldier does. The key here is the phrase, "gets entangled."

  • What does it mean to become entangled in something?

- What is the difference between taking care of legitimate daily needs and getting entangled in the pursuits of life that surround us?

- Why should we avoid that which would entangle us in order to stay faithful to Christ (the reward)? See also 2 Peter 2:20-21.

Focus on the Meaning: Believers must still live in this world and make a living to support themselves. But we should use whatever task we are engaged upon to live out and to demonstrate our Christianity… Paul's appeal shows the importance of developing an ability to distinguish between doing good things and doing the best things. Servants of Christ are not merely to be well-rounded dabblers in all types of trivial pursuits. But we are to be tough-minded devotees of Christ who constantly choose the right priorities from a list of potential selections. (*Dr. Constable's Notes on 2 Timothy 2017 Edition*, pp. 17-18)

14. Paul then turned to the image of a competitor in the Greek games (verse 5). How does being an athlete relate to being a faithful Christian?

15. The third example is that of a farmer. What does this example have to do with being a faithful Christian?

Focus on the Meaning: Paul isolated three aspects of wholeheartedness that should be found in Timothy and in us: The *dedication* of a good soldier, the law-abiding *obedience* of a good athlete, and the painstaking *labor* of a good farmer. Without these we cannot expect results. There will be no victory for the soldier unless he gives himself to his soldiering, no wreath for the athlete unless he keeps the rules, and no harvest for the farmer unless he toils at his farming. (John Stott, *Standing Firm in the Truth*)

16. How does a believer avoid getting entangled in the trappings of daily life? See 2 Timothy 1:7,14; 2:1,7; and Matthew 6:33.

What application will you make to stay faithful to God?

17. Do you consider yourself a faithful or reliable person who can "guard" the truth of Jesus Christ and teach it to others? If so, how are you taking opportunities to do this in your life?

18. It is easy to get entangled with things that are not wrong in themselves. They are wrong when they distract us from seeking first the kingdom of God. There is nothing wrong with a limited use of sports, computers, recreation or hobbies if you use them to refresh you for the battle. But it is easy for these legitimate things to suck you into the quicksand and before you know it, you're not seeking first God's kingdom.

Do you recognize some areas of entanglement that affect your dedication to serve God faithfully? Ask God to help you get untangled from at least one of them this week.

Respond to the Lord about what He's shown you today.

Day Three Study

Read 2 Timothy 2:1-13.

Ask the Lord Jesus to teach you through His Word.

The context of 2 Timothy 2 is staying faithful even in the midst of suffering. There is a reward for staying faithful.

19. After reading vv. 1-7, Paul's next words should also motivate Timothy to stay faithful. Of what does Paul remind his beloved son in vv. 8-10?

Historical Insight: Under Nero's persecution, many non-Christians viewed Christians as serious criminals. Timothy needed to remember that the Word of God was just as powerful to change lives as ever. Its power was as great as it ever was—even though one of its champion defenders was in chains. As the hymn, A Mighty Fortress Is Our God, says, "The body they may kill; God's truth abideth still; His kingdom is forever." (*Dr. Constable's Notes on 2 Timothy 2023 Edition,* p. 30)

A popular saying

Verses 11-13 are likely an early Christian hymn. The context of this whole chapter, and even the whole letter of 2ⁿᵈ Timothy, is staying faithful to Christ until "that day" when there will be a reward for doing so (2 Timothy 1:12,18). There are rewards for staying faithful as in the soldier, athlete, and farmer in 2 Timothy 2:3-6 whose rewards are a satisfied commander, victor's crown and a share of the harvest. The opposite to staying faithful (having strong faith) is becoming unfaithful (having weak faith) to Christ and losing the rewards.

One of the biggest problems the church was facing at that time was that of Christians, being gripped with fear, denying Christ in front of their tormentors and agreeing to worship Caesar in order to save their own lives.

Remember that our salvation is achieved by grace through faith alone. Paul reinforces this in 2 Timothy 1:8-11. We receive the very life of Christ as He comes to permanently live inside of us through His Holy Spirit. In essence, when God looks upon us, He sees His Son Jesus. We are members of His body. Once we have trusted in Christ, we are no longer judged by our sins. But our works are judged, and we receive rewards in heaven based on that. The context of this passage is rewards.

Scriptural Insight: If the believer departs from following Christ faithfully during his or her life (i.e., apostatizes), Christ will deny him or her at the judgment seat of Christ (Matt. 10:33; Mark 8:38; Luke 12:9; cf. Luke 19:22; Matt. 22:13; cf. Matt. 25:41-46).5 The unfaithful believer will not lose his salvation (1 John 5:13) or all of his reward (1 Pet. 1:4), but he will lose some of his reward (1 Cor. 3:12-15; cf. Luke 19:24-26). (*Dr. Constable's Notes on 2 Timothy 2023 Edition,* p. 32)

Now, we can look at verses 11-13 with greater understanding.

20. The first two couplets refer to those who are faithful and the rewards they receive. What are the choices and rewards?

    If we have died with Him, we will also live with Him. If we endure, we will also reign with Him.

> **Focus on the Meaning:** The best of life on Earth is a glimpse of Heaven; the worst of life is a glimpse of Hell. For Christians, this present life is the closest they will come to Hell. For unbelievers, it is the closest they will come to Heaven. (Randy Alcorn, *Heaven*)

The last two couplets refer to those who deny Christ (are unfaithful) and the consequences (loss of reward). Let's look at them separately.

21. *If we deny Him, He will also deny us. (end of v. 12)*

- What does it mean to "deny" someone something?

Read Luke 22:31-34 and 54-62. The same word translated "deny" was used of Peter.

- Jesus warned Peter about the temptation to deny Him (vv. 31-34). What did Peter choose to do after being warned about his denial (vv. 54-62)?

- What do you think he lost as a result of his choice?

- What did Jesus tell him to do after he repented from that choice (v. 32)?

> **Focus on the Meaning:** We know "deny" cannot mean to lose one's salvation because our salvation is based on God's grace not our works (2 Timothy 1:9). It is possible, however, for persecution to surface those who are pretending to be Christians but

have never placed their faith in Jesus Christ. We will see examples in 2 Timothy 3 of these "fakers" who have no faith in Christ.

22. *If we are faithless (unfaithful), He will remain faithful for He cannot deny Himself. (v. 13)*

- What does it mean to be faithless (literally, "betray a trust")?

- Read Galatians 2:20. How does this contribute to our understanding of v. 13?

- What is the promise to us even if we fail and are unfaithful to Him in a time of suffering?

What application will you make to stay faithful to God?

23. Persecution tests the believer's commitment to Christ.

- Of what was Paul convinced (2 Timothy 1:12)? Do you have this same conviction and commitment to Christ?

- What have you learned in this lesson that might help you go through a time of intense persecution or even imprisonment for your faith?

Respond to the Lord about what He's shown you today.

Recommended: Listen to "Staying Faithful No Matter the Cost" at melanienewton.com/podcasts after doing this lesson to reinforce what you have learned. Use the listener guide on the next page.

Staying Faithful No Matter the Cost

"Whoever wants to be my disciple must deny themselves and take up their cross and follow me. For whoever wants to save their life will lose it, but whoever loses their life for me and for the gospel will save it." (Mark 8:34-35)

As Paul was writing this letter, the Roman Emperor Nero had begun an all-out assault on Christians. Many Christians were arrested and put to death in very gruesome ways. Some Christians, being gripped with fear, were denying Christ in front of their tormentors and agreeing to worship Caesar in order to save their own lives. They were not choosing to stay faithful no matter the cost.

Through the past 2000 years, many Christians facing persecution have chosen to stay faithful to Jesus no matter the cost to them. We call them martyrs. Any Christian who swears to tell the truth about Jesus Christ regardless of the consequences is a witness to the truth about Jesus.

STAYING FAITHFUL REQUIRES ENDURANCE.

"For our light and momentary troubles are achieving for us an eternal glory that outweighs them all." (2 Corinthians 4:17)

- Jesus said to His followers that we will have trouble in this world. Some troubles simply come from living in this fallen world and are common to everyone—illness and natural disasters. Other troubles like persecution and rejection are related to being a child of God living in an unbelieving world. Then there are those we inflict upon ourselves because of sin still present within us—our own bad choices—or troubles that others inflict upon us because of their bad choices. Either way, we get stuck with the results. Any kind of suffering is painful.

- Jesus wants to help us not only survive a lifetime of ups and downs but also to thrive as we live through them. For that, you and I need to have something called **endurance**. But endurance is only learned when there is a challenge to our comfort.

- The Bible teaches that endurance is required to live this life and stay faithful to God no matter what. Endurance is a good word, but biblical endurance encompasses so much more. It is more related to the word perseverance. Perseverance is *holding to a course of action, a belief, or a purpose without giving way.* Staying faithful no matter what. That's the picture of biblical endurance. And biblical endurance has both purpose and reward.

Truth #1: Endurance is good for us.

Endurance in the Bible means "bearing under." It's holding up a load with staying power and stick-to-it-iveness. Endurance teaches us "staying power" for a long-term burden.

Truth #2: Endurance makes us stronger.

Bible study alone won't develop endurance. Just like load-bearing exercise makes your bones stronger, troubles that challenge your faith do that, too.

Truth #3: Endurance is necessary to grow up into maturity.

- In the process of human development, the goal is to grow up into a fully functioning, responsible adult. That involves enduring challenges of life so we will grow into maturity.

- But we don't necessarily desire endurance. We get sidetracked with our comforts and our rights. Without endurance, we become satisfied with immaturity. We have men and women refusing to grow up into maturity—in the workplace, in the home, and in the church. God's goal for us is to be mature and complete. Endurance is His tool to help us reach that goal.

Truth #4: Endurance teaches us to depend on God more than on ourselves.

- This popular saying is false teaching, "God doesn't give you more than you can handle." From 2 Corinthians 1:8-9, we learn that God allowed Paul and his co-workers to be under great pressure, far beyond their ability to endure. God's purpose was for them to rely on God more than on themselves. God definitely gives us more than we can handle on our own.

- Going through troubles is God's will for us. He allows things in our lives to challenge us, to develop endurance in us. It is not so we don't need Him any longer but that we would rely on Him more.

- God gives everyone more than we can handle on our own in order to drive us to Him, to rely on Him, and to gain the confidence in Him so that we will depend on Him more. Endurance teaches us to depend on God more than on ourselves.

THE PURPOSE AND THE REWARD OF ENDURANCE THROUGH SUFFERING

- Paul looked at everything he endured during his whole adult life and still saw purpose. The purpose was the salvation of many. And he reminded Timothy that though he might be chained, God's word is not chained. The gospel is not chained. The purpose for enduring the present suffering had not changed. It was to stay faithful to Jesus Christ and His gospel no matter what. *2 Timothy 2:8-10*

- He also saw the reward of staying faithful was the eternal glory he would receive when he was greeted by his Savior in heaven. We have that same reward waiting for us as believers in Christ.

- What we get now are these: staying power for a long-term burden, stronger spiritual bones, mature faith that represents Christ well on this earth, the strength of the Lord on us as we depend upon Him more than on ourselves, and opportunities to love those who hear the gospel and believe in Jesus Christ because of our witness.

Let Jesus satisfy your heart with His faithfulness. Then, make the choice to stay faithful to Him for the rest of your life.

5: Faith-Building Words

2 Timothy 2:14-26

DAY ONE STUDY—GET THE BIG PICTURE

What does the Bible say?

Ask the Lord Jesus to teach you through His Word.

Read the Bible passage below (NIV, including verses from the last lesson). Use your own method (colored pencils, lines, shapes) to mark 1) anything that grabs your attention, 2) words you want to understand, and 3) anything repeated in this passage or from a previous part of the letter. Draw arrows between thoughts that connect. Put a star ✱ next to anything you think relates to being faithful.

2 8 Remember Jesus Christ, raised from the dead, descended from David. This is my gospel, 9 for which I am suffering even to the point of being chained like a criminal. But God's word is not chained. 10 Therefore I endure everything for the sake of the elect, that they too may obtain the salvation that is in Christ Jesus, with eternal glory.

14 Keep reminding God's people of these things. Warn them before God against quarreling about words; it is of no value, and only ruins those who listen. 15 Do your best to present yourself to God as one approved, a worker who does not need to be ashamed and who correctly handles the word of truth. 16 Avoid godless chatter, because those who indulge in it will become more and more ungodly. 17 Their teaching will spread like gangrene. Among them are Hymenaeus and Philetus, 18 who have departed from the truth. They say that the resurrection has already taken place, and they destroy the faith of some. 19 Nevertheless, God's solid foundation stands firm, sealed with this inscription: "The Lord knows those who are his," and, "Everyone who confesses the name of the Lord must turn away from wickedness."

20 In a large house there are articles not only of gold and silver, but also of wood and clay; some are for special purposes and some for common use. 21 Those who cleanse themselves from the latter will be instruments for special purposes, made holy, useful to the Master and prepared to do any good work.

22 Flee the evil desires of youth and pursue righteousness, faith, love and peace, along with those who call on the Lord out of a pure heart. 23 Don't have anything to do with foolish and stupid arguments, because you know they produce quarrels. 24 And the Lord's servant must not be quarrelsome but must be kind to everyone, able to teach, not resentful. 25 Opponents must be gently instructed, in the hope that God will grant them repentance leading them to a knowledge of the truth, 26 and that they will come to their senses and escape from the trap of the devil, who has taken them captive to do his will.

1. What grabbed your attention from these verses?

2. What verses or specific words do you want to understand better?

3. What topics are repeated in this passage or continue an earlier discussion in this letter?

4. What verses illustrate or help you understand what staying faithful looks like?

5. From this lesson's passage, choose one verse to dwell upon all week long. Write it in the space below. Ask God to teach you through this verse.

Respond to the Lord about what He's shown you today.

DAY TWO STUDY

Read 2 Timothy 2:2-6 and 14-26.

Ask the Lord Jesus to teach you through His Word.

What does it mean?

Paul continues to deal with the issue of false teachers. These people caused strife and division within the new church by their meaningless quarreling over their own ideas. Paul dealt with the same issue regarding foolish arguments and godless chatter in 1 Timothy 1:3-7. In 2 Timothy chapter 2, he warns Timothy not to be "drawn into" debates with these people. Remember that the context of this whole chapter 2 is to stay faithful and not become unfaithful.

6. In the following verses, note the instruction that Paul gives to Timothy regarding what kind of "conversation" to avoid and why. Note: The "them" in v. 14 is the same as the reliable people teaching others in v. 2.

	Avoid what?	Why?
Verse 14		
Verse 16		
Verse 23		

From the Greek: The Greek phrase translated "godless chatter" refers to profane, empty discussion of vain and useless matters." "Foolish and stupid arguments (v. 23)" refers to speculations, hypotheticals, and useless debates. To "quarrel" means to contend about words, wrangle about empty and trifling matters.

7. Based on your answers above, how do you discern the difference between foolish arguments and standing up to false teaching?

8. What kind of talk in the church today would be considered quarreling about vain and useless matters? Again, consider the effect on those listening.

Think About It: Sometimes the translations we use can cause us to quarrel about words. Remember that the Scriptures were originally written in Hebrew and Greek. Our English translations have only existed since the 1600s. Over the years, they vary as word meanings change and as older manuscripts are discovered to help translators understand what the original words used by the authors meant. Choose a reliable translation for your study. Then, compare translations of specific verses to add understanding. Be aware that there are English translations that intentionally twist the Scriptures to match what the culture wants them to say. Those reflect godless chatter.

9. Although Paul instructs Timothy and the reliable teachers in the church to not engage in quarrelsome talk, he realizes that it will surface within the church. Looking at verses 24-26:

   • Under whose influence are quarrelsome people operating (v. 26)?

   • What attitude is the Lord's servant to have towards the opposition?

   • What actions should she take?

   • What is the goal of adopting such an attitude? What is God's desire for them? (See also 1 Timothy 2:3-4 and Titus 2:14.)

   From the Greek: The emphasis in the word translated "able to teach" (v. 24) in the Greek (*didaktikos*) is on the teacher's ability to bring out the best in his students rather than the teacher's knowledge. ... The Lord's servant must seek to communicate this truth in such a way that opponents embrace it and abandon their error with proper remorse. God's servant thus seeks to be the instrument through whose efforts God brings them to himself. (*Dr. Constable's Notes on 2 Timothy 2017 Edition*, pp. 27-28)

What application will you make to stay faithful to God?

10. In a group setting, women may say things that are controversial or simply untrue. What questions do you ask yourself (or should you ask yourself) to determine whether you need to stand up to false teaching or divert attention away from the comment and focus the group back to the lesson or main discussion?

11. Civil discussion of both sides of an issue is not quarreling, but it can lead to quarreling if you are not careful. Quarreling is sin, plain and simple, because it focuses on self. Consider your tendency to quarrel or argue with people (spouse, neighbor, co-worker, family member, child, someone at church).

- How do you recognize when a discussion is becoming an argument?

- When you find yourself getting caught in a quarrel or argument, stop. Do not continue. Ask the Lord to help you with this.

Respond to the Lord about what He's shown you today.

DAY THREE STUDY

Read 2 Timothy 2:14-26.

Ask the Lord Jesus to teach you through His Word.

What does it mean?

12. In 2 Timothy 2:15, how are we to present ourselves to God?

13. What does Paul's use of the phrase "do your best" imply?

14. How can any Christian (including you) handle God's Word...?

- Correctly —

- Incorrectly —

15. In vv. 17-18, what are the two men falsely teaching and with what results?

Scriptural Insight: Remember that the teaching about Jesus' resurrection and the future resurrection of all believers was new to the Gentiles. The Greeks thought the physical body was evil. Why would anyone want a new physical body? So the bodily resurrection of Jesus was foolishness to them. Hymenaeus (referenced in 1 Timothy 1:19-20) and Philetus may have been leaders of false teaching in Ephesus denying the bodily resurrection. In 1 Corinthians 15:12-19, Paul addressed similar false teaching denying the bodily resurrection of Jesus.

Another possibility is that those who heard Paul's teaching that believers now participate in the death and resurrection of Christ (Romans 6:4-5, 8) understood that to mean that the resurrection of believers had already occurred in a spiritual sense. Whether or not these men were true Christians, it is possible for genuine believers to believe and teach false doctrine like these men were doing. The fruit of their teaching showed that it was not correct because it destroyed the faith of the listeners.

16. Paul is in prison, but "God's Word is not chained" (2:9). Continuing this confidence in spite of some who are teaching lies, what Old Testament truths does Paul quote in 2:19?

17. Paul illustrates these truths in the next 2 verses. Read 2 Timothy 2:20-21. What types of "articles / vessels" are present together in a large house, and what purposes do they serve?

Focus on the Meaning: The large house is the Body of Christ, and the vessels belong to the master of the house (God). The common vessels used for chamber pots, slop buckets, and refuse would not be used by the master for eating, drinking, or displaying (noble purposes). Every Christian is set apart (sanctified) for God's special use at the moment of salvation—cleansed and made holy in our position before God. However, we are also being sanctified daily (set apart from sinful behaviors) as we choose to yield to God's Spirit working in us. What is clean and set apart for special use can easily get contaminated and rendered unusable through contact with wickedness. Everyone who confesses the name of the Lord can choose to fill their "cleansed vessel" with the holiness of God or the wickedness of the world (vv. 21-22). In our heavenly future, we will be completely sanctified, never to get dirty again!

18. What three qualities characterize a "vessel" that stays away from any impurities / wickedness that would contaminate it (end of v. 21)?

19. How can you stay a faithful vessel dedicated to God's purpose (v. 22)?

What application will you make to stay faithful to God?

20. Think of someone you know who knows how to correctly handle the Word of Truth. How did he/she cultivate this ability? (If you don't know, you might ask.) Discuss at least one step you can take to bring you closer to the goal of correctly handling God's Word.

21. Keeping in mind 2 Timothy 2:19, 22:

- How can you be a vessel faithful to Jesus that stays "set apart" and used for his noblest purposes?

- If your life has NOT been one used for God's noble purposes, maybe you are feeling worthless. Remember you belong to the Lord. He knows it. He still welcomes you with open, loving arms. If you haven't done so already, repent (turn away) from your independence from God and offer Him your life. He will take your willing heart and renew you through the Holy Spirit, redirect your life, and use it for His glory and honor!

Respond to the Lord about what He's shown you today.

Recommended: Listen to "Staying Faithful through Your Words" at melanienewton.com/podcasts after doing this lesson to reinforce what you have learned. Use the listener guide on the next page.

Staying Faithful through Your Words

In this section of Paul's letter to Timothy, he told his friend to warn the Ephesian believers against quarreling about words. He said that such quarreling is of no value and only ruins those who listen. Then, he warned Timothy to avoid godless chatter, because those who indulge in it will become more and more ungodly. Words matter. And so often, we take on the world's words in our communications, especially on social media. We have knee jerk reactions and post things that are more worldly and self-centered than godly and Christ-centered. Our words can draw the listener or the reader closer to Christ or push her further away from Christ. In our words, we are to stay faithful and useful to God.

DON'T LET ANY UNWHOLESOME TALK COME OUT OF YOUR MOUTH.

> *"Do not let any unwholesome talk come out of your mouths, but only what is helpful for building others up according to their needs, that it may benefit those who listen." (Ephesians 4:29)*

- The underlying Greek word for "unwholesome talk" means, "rotten." Rotten talk is anything that isn't beneficial for the building up of the one who is listening (or reading). Foul and abusive. Unkind, accusing, malicious, making others cringe or cry—those are unwholesome.

Toxic talk about people

- Toxic talk is laced with harsh criticism. It plants seeds of doubt about others so that distrust and hurt feelings prevail based on gossip and slander.

- Even Christians can spew such rotten talk from their mouths.

- We as believers are to stay useful to God in how we use our words. At work or any group situation, do not let any unwholesome talk come out of your mouth in the way of toxic talk about the other people.

Grumbling and arguing

> *"Do everything without grumbling or arguing," (Philippians 2:14)*

- Grumbling springs from a bad attitude expressed in muttering, whining, & griping. Arguing or quarreling springs from an arrogant attitude that starts out as grumbling then leads to outright disputes.

- Women have a tendency to mutter, grumble, whine, and gripe. And our relationships often feel the brunt of our "ungrateful" and "discontented" attitudes. Whining about life is not very effective for changing anything. Stop whining and start befriending.

- There is a difference between complaining and seeing a problem and working toward a solution. When it is possible to change the outcome of a situation, we should take action.

SPEAK HELPFUL AND BENEFICIAL WORDS

- Helpful words build others up. They strengthen them in their faith and promote their spiritual growth. Building others up according to their needs means you are paying attention to their lives and their needs.

- Our words should give grace to those who hear. Our God has lavished His grace upon us and calls us to be grace givers to others. Yet, we more quickly judge and criticize others than assume good will from them. And if wounded, we want to fight back, spewing venom to make sure everyone knows we've been hurt.

- God calls us to be grace givers, not only for the benefit of others, but because it's what is best for us! Through Christ living in us, we can take the grace God has lavished upon us and pour it back on someone else that it may "benefit those who listen."

WORDS ARE A HEART ISSUE.

- Words are a heart issue. Jesus said in Mark 7:21 that evil thoughts, malicious words, slander, and arrogance spew from the heart. *The Message* translation says those things "vomit" from the heart. What a vivid picture! By spewing such filth in her words, a Christian is revealing a heart that is not committed to obeying her Lord in this area. It's not the mouth that malfunctions. It's the heart!

- Christians over the years have learned that certain practices such as daily devotionals, dedicated prayer, and giving to others will help to keep the heart turned toward God. These are often called "spiritual disciplines." Such disciplines may heighten your sensitivity to the Holy Spirit's work in conforming your inner and outer self to look more like Jesus. What makes something a 'spiritual discipline' is that it takes a specific part of your way of life and turns it toward God. The practice of using beneficial, grace-giving speaking, texting, emailing, and writing should be considered a spiritual discipline.

- If you find yourself in a situation with another Christian where you are splattered with vicious and rotten words, I suggest you quote Ephesians 4:29 and respond, "Want to try that again?" Do the same if you hear rotten words come out of your mouth. Apologize and try it again.

Let Jesus satisfy your heart with His faithfulness. Then, make the choice to stay faithful to Him for the rest of your life.

6: Influential Fakers

2 Timothy 3:1-13

DAY ONE STUDY—GET THE BIG PICTURE

What does the Bible say?

Ask the Lord Jesus to teach you through His Word.

Read the Bible passage below (NIV, including verses from the last lesson). Use your own method (colored pencils, lines, shapes) to mark 1) anything that grabs your attention, 2) words you want to understand, and 3) anything repeated in this passage or from a previous part of the letter. Draw arrows between thoughts that connect. Put a star ✱ next to anything you think relates to being faithful.

2 22 *Flee the evil desires of youth and pursue righteousness, faith, love and peace, along with those who call on the Lord out of a pure heart. 23 Don't have anything to do with foolish and stupid arguments, because you know they produce quarrels. 24 And the Lord's servant must not be quarrelsome but must be kind to everyone, able to teach, not resentful. 25 Opponents must be gently instructed, in the hope that God will grant them repentance leading them to a knowledge of the truth, 26 and that they will come to their senses and escape from the trap of the devil, who has taken them captive to do his will.*

3 *But mark this: There will be terrible times in the last days. 2 People will be lovers of themselves, lovers of money, boastful, proud, abusive, disobedient to their parents, ungrateful, unholy, 3 without love, unforgiving, slanderous, without self-control, brutal, not lovers of the good, 4 treacherous, rash, conceited, lovers of pleasure rather than lovers of God— 5 having a form of godliness but denying its power. Have nothing to do with such people.*

6 They are the kind who worm their way into homes and gain control over gullible women, who are loaded down with sins and are swayed by all kinds of evil desires, 7 always learning but never able to come to a knowledge of the truth. 8 Just as Jannes and Jambres opposed Moses, so also these teachers oppose the truth. They are men of depraved minds, who, as far as the faith is concerned, are rejected. 9 But they will not get very far because, as in the case of those men, their folly will be clear to everyone.

10 You, however, know all about my teaching, my way of life, my purpose, faith, patience, love, endurance, 11 persecutions, sufferings—what kinds of things happened to me in Antioch, Iconium and Lystra, the persecutions I endured. Yet the Lord rescued me from all of them. 12 In fact, everyone who wants to live a godly life in Christ Jesus will be persecuted,13 while evildoers and impostors will go from bad to worse, deceiving and being deceived.

1. What grabbed your attention from these verses?

2. What verses or specific words do you want to understand better?

3. What topics are repeated in this passage or continue an earlier discussion in this letter?

4. What verses illustrate or help you understand what staying faithful looks like?

5. From this lesson's passage, choose one verse to dwell upon all week long. Write it in the space below. Ask God to teach you through this verse.

Respond to the Lord about what He's shown you today.

DAY TWO STUDY

Read 2 Timothy 3:1-13.

Ask the Lord Jesus to teach you through His Word.

What does it mean?

In his previous letter, Paul had given Timothy some instruction concerning those who will abandon the faith in the last days. The phrase "last days" includes the entire period between the first century and Christ's return for His own at the Rapture (1 Thessalonians 4:15-17). They are "last" not because they are few but because they are the final days of the present age. Jesus referred to this period as the UNTIL time in Luke 21:24, "until the times of the Gentiles be fulfilled." Here as well as in Romans 1:28-32, Paul gives a list of general human behaviors that have existed throughout history but will increase in scope and acceptance over time. All of these will contribute to the suffering of Christians who are trying to stay faithful to the Lord.

6. In 2 Timothy 3:1, Paul says the last days will be difficult. What will characterize the last days to make it so difficult (vv. 2-4)?

> **Dependent Living:** Wondering how to live in such difficult times? In 2ⁿᵈ Timothy chapters 1 and 2, Paul has already described how to rely on God during such times, how to stay faithful to Him, and how to focus on the reward for doing so.

7. Read Acts 20:28-31. Ten years before writing 2ⁿᵈ Timothy, Paul met with the Ephesian elders and warned them about savage wolves infiltrating the flock. Paul continues to warn Timothy (and us) about savage wolves but in different terms.

    *   How are they described in 2 Timothy 3:5?

    *   How are they described in Titus 1:16?

    *   What could Paul mean by saying "having a form of godliness but denying its power?"

8. As we look at vv. 5-7, we see that Paul is describing "influential fakers." They are not Christians (v. 8). They just look like "good people."

    *   Why would Paul say to not associate with them?

- What would it look like to not associate with them?

The ungodly fakers seek to influence. They will look for the best means of influence and seek targets that are easily influenced.

9. Look at the first part of verse 6. The NIV translators used a word picture for us that we can recognize, "worm their way into homes." This is a means for the influential fakers to reach their targets. After reading the "Focus on the Meaning" below, what could that look like?

> **Focus on the Meaning:** "Worm their way into homes/households" means to sneak in, to introduce yourself gradually and cunningly into a position, especially a place of confidence or favor. "To gain control over" means to make a prisoner of, take captive especially thoughts and emotions as in 2 Timothy 2:26.

10. Read vv. 6-7 in 3 translations. What words did Paul use to describe the targets of these influential fakers?

> **Focus on the Meaning:** The phrase "weak-willed women" is literally "little women," which is referring to someone who is silly and vulnerable, the opposite of someone who is wise. Although Paul used women as an example, the vulnerability applies to men as well as to women. In their unguardedness, they open the door and let the fakers inside.

11. Let's focus on the phrase "loaded down (heaped on, overwhelmed) with sins."

- How do women get loaded down with sins?

- How might this make them feel and, therefore, be vulnerable?

- How do they try to deal with their guilt?

- What truth do they need to know that would free them from being overwhelmed by sin?

12. What does it mean that they are "swayed (led along, taken by the hand) by all kinds of evil desires"?

13. What would it look like to be "always learning but never able to acknowledge (arrive at, be established upon) the truth?" See also 2 Timothy 4:3-4.

> **Scriptural Insight:** Paul gives 2 examples of influential fakers in 2 Timothy 3:8-9. Paul mentions two characters, Jannes and Jambres, whose names mean "he who seduces" and "he who is rebellious." Neither name is in the Old Testament, but Jewish legend held that these were the names of 2 Egyptian magicians who opposed Moses' demand of Pharaoh to free the Israelites (Exodus 7:11-12, 22). They tried to duplicate the miracles of Moses in an attempt to discredit him. But God showed that Moses' authority was more powerful. (*The Word in Life Study Bible*, p. 751)

What application will you make to stay faithful to God?

14. How might such influential fakers "worm their way into homes" today? What do you do to protect yourself and your household from influential fakers?

15. Do you know any women who fit the description Paul gave in vv. 6-7?

   • If you do, how can you come alongside to help her?

   • What can you do if she doesn't want to change?

16. Does 2 Timothy 3:1-9 offer any warnings you think you should heed? If so, what are those warnings? What will you ask God to do in your life so that none of the negative behaviors characterize you?

Respond to the Lord about what He's shown you today.

DAY THREE STUDY

Read 2 Timothy 3:1-13.

Ask the Lord Jesus to teach you through His Word.

Paul compares his example to the influential fakers. Timothy knows Paul well.

17. Considering the threat of betrayal and persecution by the Romans, why is Paul reminding Timothy of what he learned from Paul's example about following Christ and staying faithful to Him during difficult times (vv. 10-11)?

18. During Paul's previous times of "persecutions" and "sufferings," what did God do for him?

Scriptural Insight: Timothy probably met Paul when the apostle first arrived in Lystra (Acts 14:8-23). Before this, some Jews had already run Paul and Barnabas out of Pisidian Antioch and Iconium for preaching about Jesus. But Lystra warmly welcomed the missionaries until Jews from Antioch and Iconium arrived and persuaded the Lystrians to turn against Paul and Barnabas. The crowd stoned Paul and dragged Paul's body outside the city, presuming he was dead. But Paul survived, and after spending some time in Derbe he returned to strengthen the disciples in Lystra. "We must go through many hardships to enter the kingdom of God," Paul reminded the Lystrian believers (Acts 14:22). (*2 Timothy Life Change Bible Study*, pg.60)

19. According to 2 Timothy 3:12,

    • Who will be persecuted?

    • Why is this so? See John 15:18-25 and 2 Timothy 3:2-4, 13.

Scriptural Insight: Timothy needed to realize, as all Christians do, that when a person determines to "live a godly life," [she] will suffer persecution. With her commitment to follow Christ faithfully, [she] sets the course of her life directly opposite to the course of the world system. Confrontation and conflict become inevitable. (*Dr. Constable's Notes on 2 Timothy 2017 Edition*, p. 32)

20. But God uses persecution to be something "good" for us. Read 2 Corinthians 1:9; 4:7-9; and 12:9-10. Why is depending upon Him more than on ourselves "good" for us?

Dependent Living: Human parents raise their children to be less dependent on them and more independent. But God raises His children to be *less independent* and ***more dependent on Him.*** Whatever He brings into our lives that makes us more dependent upon Him is good for us. When you are persecuted or perceive a threat of it, remember also that there is a reward for staying faithful (2 Timothy 2:3-6, 12).

What application will you make to stay faithful to God?

From what we have learned so far in 2 Timothy, our first response during persecution is to Christ (2 Timothy 1:12), staying faithful to Him because we are confident in who He is and how much He loves us. Our second response is to the opposition (2 Timothy 2:24-26) with our words and our behavior. See "Dangerous Times for Christians" after the next question.

21. When you have been persecuted for being a Christian, or perceived the threat of it,

- How have you responded in the past?

- What would you do differently next time, if anything?

DANGEROUS TIMES FOR CHRISTIANS

(The commentary below is adapted from "Truth and Tolerance" by Josh McDowell, *Focus on the Family,* August 1999)

One of the ways our western culture persecutes Christians is through the redefinition of tolerance. The traditional definition of tolerance means simply to recognize and respect others' beliefs, practices, and so forth without necessarily agreeing or sympathizing with them.

But today's new "tolerance" considers every individual's beliefs, values, lifestyle, and truth claims as equally valid. So not only does everyone have an equal right to his beliefs, but all beliefs are equal. The new tolerance goes beyond respecting a person's rights; it demands praise and endorsement of that person's beliefs, values, and lifestyle.

The results of the new tolerance:

- The repression of public discourse. "How dare you say that?" The issue is no longer the truth of the message, but the right to proclaim it. In the new cultural climate, any unpopular message can be labeled "intolerant" and therefore be repressed.

- The privatization of convictions. Christians face increasing pressure to be silent about their convictions - in school, at work, in the public square - because to speak out will be seen as an intolerant judgement of others' beliefs and lifestyles.

- A new wave of religious persecution. Linking so-called "hate crimes" to intolerance.

What does the Lord require?

It is not too late to avoid such scenarios, but I believe doing so will require effort in these areas:

WE MUST HUMBLY PURSUE TRUTH.

Pursuing truth in this context means embracing all people, but not all beliefs. It means listening to and learning from all people without necessarily agreeing with them. "But do this with gentleness and respect" (1 Peter 3:15).

WE MUST AGGRESSIVELY PRACTICE LOVE.

Love actively seeks to promote the good of another person.

Tolerance says:	Love responds with doing something harder:
"You must approve of what I do."	"I will love you, even when your behavior offends me."
"You must agree with me."	"I will tell you the truth, because I am convinced, 'the truth will set you free.'
"You must allow me to have my way."	"I will plead with you to follow the right way, because I believe you are worth the risk."

Tolerance seeks to be inoffensive; love takes risks. Tolerance glorifies division; love seeks unity. Tolerance costs nothing; love costs everything.

Respond to the Lord about what He's shown you today.

Recommended: Listen to "Staying Faithful through Grasping Truth" at melanienewton.com/podcasts after doing this lesson to reinforce what you have learned. Use the listener guide on the next page.

Staying Faithful through Grasping Truth

WHAT TAKES WOMEN CAPTIVE TO SPIRITUAL ERROR?

"They are the kind who worm their way into homes and gain control over gullible women, who are loaded down with sins and are swayed by all kinds of evil desires, always learning but never able to come to a knowledge of the truth." (2 Timothy 3:6-7)

- False teachers are influential fakers—they look good on the outside but have no spiritual power on the inside.

- Influential fakers worm their way into homes of any woman who leaves the door open. Once inside, they gain control over the gullible, weak-willed women.

- Women become especially vulnerable to influential fakers when they are loaded down with guilt from their sins or when they are on the constant search for the latest new thing to satisfy the restlessness in their hearts. Various lusts feed their discontentment.

- Women who never recognize and grasp biblical truth will be taken captive by whatever flashy teachings that come along and live unsatisfied, unstable lives.

GRASP THIS TRUTH: BY FAITH IN JESUS CHRIST, YOUR SIN AND GUILT IS TAKEN AWAY. YOU ARE COMPLETELY FORGIVEN.

- All of our debt of sin before God is enormous. But God stepped in and did for us what we couldn't do for ourselves. He transferred our sin to a substitute, Jesus, and it was taken away.

- Once you place your faith in Jesus Christ, whatever you've done that was wrong in God's eyes from the time you were born through the time of your death has been canceled. Your forgiveness is complete and continual. *Colossians 2:13-14; Ephesians 1:7*

- As long as you live in your earthly body, sin will happen—whether intentionally or unintentionally. As an already forgiven Christian, you can follow a biblical process for dealing with recognized sin—remember first your identity as child of God, then agree with God that you've sinned against Him, mourn your sin and depend on the Holy Spirit to help you obey God in the future. Then, trust in Him to help you overcome the consequences of any sinful choices you've made in a way that brings glory to Him.

GRASP THIS TRUTH: BY FAITH IN JESUS CHRIST, YOU ARE REDEEMED, NO LONGER IN BONDAGE TO SIN AND LUSTS.

Fed by lusts

- A lust is a passionate or overmastering desire or craving for something. It is any desire, craving, or longing for what is generally forbidden or not good for you.

- Any woman who allows herself to feast on her lusts increases her discontentment with life as well as increases her guilt when she acts on that lust. The Bible describes that as being in bondage to sin as a slave master.

Released from bondage

- On the cross, Jesus paid the purchase price out of our slavery to sin with His blood (Mark 10:45). We have been **released into freedom** to serve God with our bodies and souls in obedience to Him. The Bible calls this whole process "redemption."

- Redemption means you become the possession of a loving, merciful God and can live in the security of your freedom from bondage to sin. A **greater power than sin moves in—** the Holy Spirit. He **sets you free** from the power of that old slave master.

- You have to claim that freedom whenever you get signals from your body or mind saying, "I want to do what I want to do."

GRASP THIS TRUTH: DWELLING IN THE TRUTH OF GOD PROTECTS YOU FROM BEING TAKEN CAPTIVE BY INFLUENTIAL FAKERS.

- Vulnerable women are "always learning but never able to come to a knowledge of the truth." They could not recognize the truth when they saw it.

- We can become willing participants in our own deception when we become bored by, apathetic to, or annoyed by established Christian truth—sound doctrine. *2 Timothy 4:3-4*

- Women need to not only be exposed to truth but to grasp it and hold vigorously to it so we won't be taken captive by the enemy's schemes. Dwell in the truth of God you can know. Humbly accept what you don't know or understand. And then, discern any teaching that you read or hear through the complete revelation of God's Word.

  The more we choose God's truth and God's way, the easier it becomes to resist the lies of the enemy and turn away from the temptations of the flesh. (Teasi Cannon, *Mama Bear Apologetics,* p. 91)

Let Jesus satisfy your heart with His faithfulness. Then, make the choice to stay faithful to Him for the rest of your life.

7: A Faithful Life with No Regrets

2 Timothy 3:14-4:8

DAY ONE STUDY—GET THE BIG PICTURE

What does the Bible say?

Ask the Lord Jesus to teach you through His Word.

Read the Bible passage below (NIV, including verses from the last lesson). Use your own method (colored pencils, lines, shapes) to mark 1) anything that grabs your attention, 2) words you want to understand, and 3) anything repeated in this passage or from a previous part of the letter. Draw arrows between thoughts that connect. Put a star ✱ next to anything you think relates to being faithful.

3 10 You, however, know all about my teaching, my way of life, my purpose, faith, patience, love, endurance, 11 persecutions, sufferings—what kinds of things happened to me in Antioch, Iconium and Lystra, the persecutions I endured. Yet the Lord rescued me from all of them. 12 In fact, everyone who wants to live a godly life in Christ Jesus will be persecuted,13 while evildoers and impostors will go from bad to worse, deceiving and being deceived.

14 But as for you, continue in what you have learned and have become convinced of, because you know those from whom you learned it, 15 and how from infancy you have known the Holy Scriptures, which are able to make you wise for salvation through faith in Christ Jesus. 16 All Scripture is God-breathed and is useful for teaching, rebuking, correcting and training in righteousness, 17 so that the servant of God may be thoroughly equipped for every good work.

4 In the presence of God and of Christ Jesus, who will judge the living and the dead, and in view of his appearing and his kingdom, I give you this charge: 2 Preach the word; be prepared in season and out of season; correct, rebuke and encourage—with great patience and careful instruction. 3 For the time will come when people will not put up with sound doctrine. Instead, to suit their own desires, they will gather around them a great number of teachers to say what their itching ears want to hear. 4 They will turn their ears away from the truth and turn aside to myths. 5 But you, keep your head in all situations, endure hardship, do the work of an evangelist, discharge all the duties of your ministry.

6 For I am already being poured out like a drink offering, and the time for my departure is near. 7 I have fought the good fight, I have finished the race, I have kept the faith. 8 Now there is in store for me the crown of righteousness, which the Lord, the righteous Judge, will award to me on that day—and not only to me, but also to all who have longed for his appearing.

1. What grabbed your attention from these verses?

2. What verses or specific words do you want to understand better?

3. What topics are repeated in this passage or continue an earlier discussion in this letter?

4. What verses illustrate or help you understand what staying faithful looks like?

5. From this lesson's passage, choose one verse to dwell upon all week long. Write it in the space below. Ask God to teach you through this verse.

Respond to the Lord about what He's shown you today.

DAY TWO STUDY

What does it mean?

Read 2 Timothy 3:14-4:2.

Ask the Lord Jesus to teach you through His Word.

6. Paul wants Timothy to draw strength from what he has "learned and become convinced of" (3:14). What is the difference between what you have learned and what you have become convinced of? Refer back to 2 Timothy 3:6-7.

7. What does Paul assert about the Scriptures (3:15)?

8. Read 2 Timothy 3:16-17 and 2 Peter 1:20-21. Although Paul is referring primarily to the Old Testament, the word "Scripture" applies to **all** divinely inspired writings (Old and New Testaments) as a whole. Inspiration refers to original autographs (written in Hebrew and Greek) but not to translations into other languages (Latin, German, English, etc.). Read the information below and summarize what "God breathed" means regarding the Scriptures.

> **Focus on the Meaning:** All Scripture is *divinely* "inspired" (Gr. *theopneustos*, lit. "God-breathed"). The Greek word *theopneustos* is composed of *theo*, meaning "God," and *pneustos*, which refers to "breathing, blowing, or sending forth one's spirit." It does not merely *contain* the Word of God, or *become* the Word of God under certain conditions. It *is* God's Word, the expression of His *Person* (heart, mind, will, etc.). This was the view of the Hebrew Bible that Jews in the first century commonly held. Using their own personalities, writing styles, life situations, etc., the words that the apostles and prophets wrote are from God. (Adapted from *2 Timothy Life Change Bible Study*, p. 63, *Dr. Constable's Notes on 2 Timothy 2017 Edition*, p. 34, and *NET Bible Translation Series* on Bible.org)

Summary:

> **Scriptural Insight:** Reading 1 Timothy 5:18 (quoting Luke 10:7) and 2 Peter 3:15-16 (referring to Paul's letters), you see that some material ultimately included in the New Testament was already considered equal in authority to the Old Testament Scriptures.

9. According to 2 Timothy 3:16-17, how is "God-breathed" Scripture useful or profitable to us? List the ways given in these verses, and explain what the words mean.

10. From verse 17, what is the ultimate goal of using God's Word for these purposes? See Romans 15:4 for another goal.

11. Read 2 Timothy 4:1-2, 8. Paul's final words to Timothy in this letter carried a particularly solemn charge (command or injunction). Verse 1 is like a long "therefore."

- What does Paul stress about Christ who is witnessing this charge to Timothy (4:1, 8)?

- Why would this motivate Timothy to carry out Paul's charge?

Historical Insight: "Appearing" was a meaningful term in Paul's day. "The [Roman] Emperor's appearance in any place was his *epiphaneia* ["appearing"]. Obviously when the Emperor was due to visit any place, everything was put in perfect order. The streets were swept and garnished; all work was up-to-date. The town was scoured and decorated to be fit for the *epiphaneia* of the Emperor. So Paul says to Timothy: 'You know what happens when any town is expecting the *epiphaneia* of the Emperor; *you* are expecting the *epiphaneia* of Jesus Christ. Do your work in such a way that all things will be ready whenever He appears.'" (*Dr. Constable's Notes on 2 Timothy*, p. 35)

12. Continuing his declaration from 3:16-17:

- Write out Paul's charge to Timothy in v. 2.

- Why is this also for every Christian who has a circle of influence? See 2 Timothy 2:2, 15.

Focus on the Meaning: The word translated "preach" refers to the 'herald' whose duty it was to make public proclamation. The verb thus means 'proclaim aloud, publicly' and is used in the NT of public proclamation of the message that God has given ... We are not to preach *about* the Word of God or *from* the Word of God [i.e., lifting a text from it and then weaving a message around that text], but preach the Word of God itself! (*Dr. Constable's Notes on 2 Timothy 2017 Edition,* p. 36)

13. What does "be prepared in season and out of season" mean (v. 2)?

As Timothy preached the Word of God, he would need to correct false teaching, to rebuke believers who are willingly sinning, and to encourage those sincerely trying to grow in the faith and knowledge of Jesus Christ (4:2).

14. How is a servant of Christ to interact with all of these people? See also 2 Timothy 2:15, 24-25.

What application will you make to stay faithful to God?

15. What does the truth that Scripture was actually "God-breathed" mean to you personally? What implications, or applications, does that have for you…in your teaching, your way of life, your purpose, your faith, your character…?

16. What responsibilities and tasks do you administer that require great patience and instruction? Usually, nothing good happens when you carry them out in anger and frustration. How can you apply what you have learned in this lesson to those tasks?

Respond to the Lord about what He's shown you today.

DAY THREE STUDY

What does it mean?

Read 2 Timothy 4:1-8.

Ask the Lord Jesus to teach you through His Word.

Paul's continuing concern about false teaching was a catalyst in issuing the charge in vv. 1-2 to Timothy. When Paul spoke about false teaching, he usually focused on the evil intentions of the false teachers. However, false teachers could not flourish if they had no audience. In this context, the listeners in Ephesus are believers. See 1 Timothy 4:1.

17. List the process by which they become willing participants in their own deception (vv. 3-4).

> **Focus on the Meaning:** Paul pictured people who would be bored by, apathetic to, and annoyed by "sound doctrine." In other words, they have made themselves the measure of who should teach them and what teaching is acceptable. Moreover, they would choose to believe "myths" rather than the truth. (*Dr. Constable's Notes on 2 Timothy 2017 Edition,* p. 37)

18. Paul uses a word picture of people having itchy ears and wanting them to be scratched. See other examples of this in Acts 7:51 and 17:21. The question to ask here in 2 Timothy 4 and in our own world is this, "What is causing the itch?"

19. When people reject sound doctrine, what or who are they really rejecting and why?

20. In what way do people take comfort in their own doctrine?

21. Regardless of false teaching around him, what is to be Timothy's focus so as not to be distracted (v. 5) so that he can complete the work God has given him to do (v. 2)?

22. Paul reflects on his life of staying faithful to God. How did he view what was happening (v. 6)?

> **Scriptural Insight:** A drink offering consisted of wine poured out on an altar as a sacrifice to God (Numbers 15:1-10). It was the last act of the Jewish sacrificial ceremony. Paul's view was that his life was not being taken from him; he was laying it down as a living sacrifice of worship (Romans 12:1).

23. Paul knew he would be executed soon. The time for his departure had come (v. 6).

> **From the Greek:** "Departure" translates a Greek word referring to untying a boat's ropes from the wharf so as to set sail. Isn't that a beautiful way to describe death?

- As he looked back over 30 years as Christ's servant, what did he say about his life (v. 7)?

> **From the Greek:** The word translated "kept" means to guard, to attend carefully, or to guard from loss or injury by keeping the eye upon.

- Based upon what you have learned in 2 Timothy, what does it mean to "keep the faith?"

- Why did Paul compare the task of "keeping the faith" to a "good fight" and a "race?"

> **Dependent Living:** Paul was able to "keep the faith" because he relied on the strength and power of Jesus Christ more than on himself (2 Timothy 1:7, 2:1). He depended on Christ in his weaknesses and in his strengths. We can and should do the same.

24. Looking at verse 8:

- What reward is Paul anticipating?

- Who will bestow this reward?

- To whom will this reward be given?

Scriptural Insight: The Bible describes 5 crowns in relation to believers. 1) An "imperishable crown" in 1 Corinthians 9:25 for leading a disciplined life, 2) A "crown of rejoicing" in 1 Thessalonians 2:19 for evangelism and discipleship, 3) A "crown of righteousness" in 2 Timothy 4:8 for loving the Lord's appearing, 4) A "crown of life" in James 1:12 and Revelation 2:10 for enduring trials, and 5) A "crown of glory" in 1 Peter 5:4 for shepherding God's flock faithfully. (Adapted from *Dr. Constable's Notes on 2 Timothy 2017 Edition,* p. 41)

What application will you make to stay faithful to God?

25. How do you see what Paul describes in 2 Timothy 4:3-4 taking place in our world? Do you personally know anyone like those described in verses 3-4? How will you pray for her specifically?

Or on a deeper level, was this ever a portrait of you? If so, how have you changed? To what do you attribute this change?

26. As he neared the end of his life, Paul could confidently say he had been faithful to God's call. Thus, he faced death calmly, knowing that Christ would reward him. Is your life preparing you for death? Do you share Paul's confident expectation of meeting Christ? How do Paul's words challenge your life?

Respond to the Lord about what He's shown you today.

> **Recommended:** Listen to "Staying Faithful through the Gift of People" at melanienewton.com/podcasts after doing this lesson to reinforce what you have learned. Use the listener guide on the next page.

Staying Faithful through the Gift of People

Jesus Christ is the best giver! He gives so many things to us that we don't deserve and can never earn. He gives us these gifts out of His love for us. Paul teaches this in every one of his letters we have in the New Testament.

THE GIFTS OF THE CROSS

As a direct result of Christ's finished work on the cross, our relationship with God is changed forever because of our faith in His Son. We receive much more than just having our sins forgiven and going to heaven when we die. Christ gives us mind-blowing, heart-thrilling gifts.

- Here are a few of the best gifts He has given to you and I as believers.

    - ✓ You can know that God is no longer angry at your sin because His holy wrath against sin was fully **satisfied** by Jesus' death on the cross.

    - ✓ You are given complete **reconciliation** in your relationship with God because Jesus becomes the bridge for you.

    - ✓ You are given **redemption** meaning you have been freed from the slavery to sin and released to serve God in freedom.

    - ✓ You are given complete **forgiveness** of your sins. This gift is ongoing and includes every sin—past, present, and future. God has erased your mistakes so that you are no longer guilty.

    - ✓ You receive the gift of being **declared righteous** in God's eyes so that now you are perfectly acceptable to a holy God based on your faith in His Son.

    - ✓ You receive the gift of being **sanctified**—declared holy to God and set apart by Him for His special use.

- We also receive the gift of being a new creation with a new identity in Christ. Everyone who trusts in Christ is lavished with treasure in Christ. And you get it all at once as a package deal the moment you place your faith in Jesus Christ. *Ephesians 1:3-14*

- God gives us people in our lives to cherish and strengthen us. God's gift of people who model following Christ for us help us to stay faithful to Him.

THE GIFT OF MOTHERS

God gave Timothy two special gifts in his life—his mother and grandmother—who taught him to love God and place His faith in Jesus Christ. They gave him what some would call "sticky faith." *2 Timothy 1:5; 3:14-15*

THE GIFT OF STICKY FAITH THAT LASTS

- "Sticky faith" is what parents can intentionally do to help our children have real faith that sticks beyond the time when they live in our homes.

- In *Three Common Traits of Youth Who Don't Leave the Church*, the author concluded that teens whose faith stuck throughout college and into their 20s had three things in common by the time they finished high school.

- *Common condition #1: They were born again, and they knew it.* That means they understood that at a specific time they had made a conscious decision to put their faith in Jesus Christ and to follow Him as His disciple.

- *Common condition #2: They were equipped, not entertained, as youth.* The teens with sticky faith knew how to share the gospel. They also knew how to disciple someone and lead a Bible study.

- *Common condition #3: Their parents lived the gospel before them.* More importantly, they lived out the gospel of grace rather than living by law. When you understand God's grace and live it out for all to see, others can see that you are motivated to obey God because of love and gratitude for what He has done for you. This is catching so those watching will be motivated to love God and be grateful to Him, also. Having godly parents is important, but so is having godly mentors.

- Paul was such a mentor to Timothy. Throughout both 1 and 2 Timothy, Paul encouraged the young man to keep doing what was right and keep teaching truth even if some people who hated Christians would try to stop his teaching what the Bible says. His love for Timothy oozes from both of those letters.

- Every parent knows that regardless of how much you influence them in the right direction, each child must still respond to Jesus' call on his or her life individually. So we should pray and trust in our God to capture the heart of our child as He has already captured our hearts. Then, we depend on Jesus to help us do our part and leave the rest up to Him. Once a child trusts in Christ as Savior, the best influence for "sticky faith" ever—God's Holy Spirit—moves inside to impact that child from the inside out for the rest of his or her life! Thank you, Jesus!

Let Jesus satisfy your heart with His faithfulness. Then, make the choice to stay faithful to Him for the rest of your life.

8: Stay Faithful to the End

2 Timothy 4:9-22

DAY ONE STUDY—GET THE BIG PICTURE

What does the Bible say?

Ask the Lord Jesus to teach you through His Word.

Read the Bible passage below (NIV, including verses from the last lesson). Use your own method (colored pencils, lines, shapes) to mark 1) anything that grabs your attention, 2) words you want to understand, and 3) anything repeated in this passage or from a previous part of the letter. Draw arrows between thoughts that connect. Put a star ✱ next to anything you think relates to being faithful.

4 *6 For I am already being poured out like a drink offering, and the time for my departure is near. 7 I have fought the good fight, I have finished the race, I have kept the faith. 8 Now there is in store for me the crown of righteousness, which the Lord, the righteous Judge, will award to me on that day—and not only to me, but also to all who have longed for his appearing.*

9 Do your best to come to me quickly, 10 for Demas, because he loved this world, has deserted me and has gone to Thessalonica. Crescens has gone to Galatia, and Titus to Dalmatia. 11 Only Luke is with me. Get Mark and bring him with you, because he is helpful to me in my ministry. 12 I sent Tychicus to Ephesus. 13 When you come, bring the cloak that I left with Carpus at Troas, and my scrolls, especially the parchments.

14 Alexander the metalworker did me a great deal of harm. The Lord will repay him for what he has done. 15 You too should be on your guard against him, because he strongly opposed our message.

16 At my first defense, no one came to my support, but everyone deserted me. May it not be held against them. 17 But the Lord stood at my side and gave me strength, so that through me the message might be fully proclaimed and all the Gentiles might hear it. And I was delivered from the lion's mouth. 18 The Lord will rescue me from every evil attack and will bring me safely to his heavenly kingdom. To him be glory for ever and ever. Amen.

19 Greet Priscilla and Aquila and the household of Onesiphorus. 20 Erastus stayed in Corinth, and I left Trophimus sick in Miletus. 21 Do your best to get here before winter. Eubulus greets you, and so do Pudens, Linus, Claudia and all the brothers and sisters.

22 The Lord be with your spirit. Grace be with you all.

1. What grabbed your attention from these verses?

2. What verses or specific words do you want to understand better?

3. What topics are repeated in this passage or continue an earlier discussion in this letter?

4. What verses illustrate or help you understand what staying faithful looks like?

5. From this lesson's passage, choose one verse to dwell upon all week long. Write it in the space below. Ask God to teach you through this verse.

Respond to the Lord about what He's shown you today.

DAY TWO STUDY

Read 2 Timothy 4:9-16.

Ask the Lord Jesus to teach you through His Word.

What does it mean?

6. What did Paul ask of Timothy in vv. 9, 11, 13, and 21?

Historical Insight: Winter severely restricted travel in some parts of the Roman world. Timothy needed to leave Ephesus soon, so he could reach Rome without undue difficulty.

In Paul's final words we get an intimate glimpse of his character, needs, and humanity. Although Paul had the assurance of eternal life and confidence in Christ, he felt the pain of loneliness in his situation. Let's look at those who were with Paul but were now gone.

7. Demas (v. 10). Demas was one of Paul's close associates. Read Colossians 4:14 and Philemon 24. Demas was a fellow worker known to the Colossians and had been with Paul in his first Roman imprisonment.

   • What did Paul say about Demas in 2 Timothy 4:10?

   • What could that mean?

Focus on the Meaning: Paul wrote that Demas deserted (abandoned) him. There is no indication that Demas deserted Christ. If he was afraid of being caught, Thessalonica was safer than Rome.

8. Who else did Paul mention in 2 Timothy 4:10-13, and what is said about them?

Historical Insight: Nothing is known about Crescens, except he was dispatched elsewhere by Paul for God's service. Titus was a close friend who aided Paul in two crises and pastored the church at Crete. Luke was a doctor who accompanied Paul on his missionary journeys and had shared the first Roman imprisonment with him (Colossians 4:14; Philippians 24). He wrote the books of Luke and Acts. Mark had left Paul and Barnabas on their first missionary journey (Acts 15:36-40). Paul now considered him helpful in his ministry. Tychicus was a close companion of Paul (Acts 20:4). He carried Paul's letters to the Ephesians, the Colossians, and Titus (see Ephesians 6:21; Colossians 4:7 and Titus 3:12).

9. Alexander the metalworker (vv. 14-15). The name Alexander is mentioned twice regarding Paul's ministry (Acts 19:23-33; 1 Timothy 1:19-20). Perhaps this Alexander is the same one.

   - What does Paul say about him?

   - What is Paul's exhortation to Timothy regarding this man?

10. Paul seemed to understand the fear that gripped the Roman Christians. What was his response towards these friends and companions who abandoned him (v. 16)?

    Historical Insight: In 2 Timothy 4:16 Paul talks about his "first defense." This was most likely a preliminary hearing (leading up to his present trial) at which advocates for the accused person were usually heard. The Roman legal system allowed for several steps in the prosecution of an accused criminal. But in Paul's case, no one came to speak in his defense or to stand by him in support. Everyone had abandoned him (see also 2 Timothy 1:15). Under emperor Nero, it was dangerous to be a Christian in Rome. Identifying oneself with the courageous and outspoken apostle Paul would almost certainly result in imprisonment along with him and certain death.

What application will you make to stay faithful to God?

11. Paul exemplified one of the toughest tasks a Christian may have to do—to leave his/her hurt with the Lord.

    - Do you recall a time when you felt abandoned by your family and/or friends? What happened? How did their neglect affect you?

- When others oppose you and undercut your authority or desert you, what is your natural response? How could this natural response damage you more than the person inflicting such pain?

- Read Romans 12:17-20 and 2 Timothy 2:24-26 for the proper response. How do these verses motivate you to bring your emotions in line with Biblical truth when you've been deeply wounded by someone?

Focus on the Meaning: Paul strongly advocated being a 'peace'-maker, but he did not promote peace *at any price*. In some situations, peace might give way to conflict if, for example, the truth is at stake (as we have seen in 2nd Timothy). In any case, the believer should not be the instigator of trouble under normal circumstances. If hostility does erupt, the Christian should not retaliate ("not take . . . revenge"). Rather, he or she should trust God to right the wrong ... The expression "heaping burning coals on his head" supposedly alludes to the old custom of carrying burning coals in a pan. When one's fire went out at home, a person would have to go to a neighbor and request hot coals that he or she would then carry home in a pan, typically on the head. Carrying the coals involved some danger, discomfort, and uneasiness for the person carrying them. Nevertheless, they were the evidence of the neighbor's love. (*Dr. Constable's Notes on Romans 2014 Edition*, p. 154)

Respond to the Lord about what He's shown you today.

DAY THREE STUDY

Read 2 Timothy 4:9-22.

Ask the Lord Jesus to teach you through His Word.

What does it mean?

Focus on 2 Timothy 4:16-18.

> **From the Greek:** "Strengthened" (v. 17) comes from the Greek word meaning "infuse with strength."

12. During that hour of darkness, who stood with Paul to strengthen him, and for what purpose (v. 17)?

13. Look at Paul's mission from Jesus in Acts 9:15-16; 22:14-15; and 26:16-20. Has anything changed even though 30 years have passed and Paul is an old man?

14. What had Jesus promised to His apostles in Matthew 10:17-20?

15. Before this time, when had Jesus stood by Paul and what did Jesus say to him then?

   • Acts 22:17-21—

   • Acts 18:9-10 —

   • Acts 23:11 —

   Summarize how Jesus consistently infused Paul with strength.

16. What was the temporary outcome for Paul after his hearing (v. 17)?

> **Focus on the Meaning:** "Delivered out of the lion's mouth (v.18)" Some have seen this as a reference to Nero throwing Christians to the lions in the Coliseum, or perhaps to Satan (for a parallel, see 1 Peter 5:8). More likely, Paul used a common biblical metaphor describing deliverance from extreme danger (see, for example, Psalm 22:21; Daniel 6:22). Paul knew he wouldn't get out of prison alive, though he was experiencing a temporary reprieve due to a delay in the Roman judicial system. (*Life Application Bible Commentary*)

17. How does Paul view his impending death / departure and what would happen (vv. 6, 18)?

Paul was considering the coming heavenly kingdom as he wrote 2 Timothy 4:1-18, especially verses 1 and 18. Paul was likely referring to the way all Christians will participate in Christ's rule when they enter His presence. That will include His millennial reign on the earth.

18. Paul's confidence in and appreciation of God is absolute, despite his cruel circumstances. Just as Paul praised God in life, what does he write in the face of death (end of v. 18)?

Final words

Focus on 2 Timothy 4:19-22.

19. What do you learn about Paul's friends and associates from the following verses? We will see them in heaven one day. ☺

- Priscilla and Aquila (v. 19): Read Acts 18:2-3, 18-19, 24-26; Romans 16:3; and 1 Corinthians 16:19.

- Onesiphorus (v. 19): Review also what is said about him in 2 Timothy 1:16-18.

- Erastus (v. 20): Read Acts 19:22; Romans 16:23.

- Trophimus (v. 20): Read Acts 20:4; 21:29.

Historical Insight: The rest are likely members of the church in Rome. Linus may have been the first bishop of Rome following the martyrdom of Peter and Paul.

20. What are Paul's final words in v. 22, which are also words for you?

What application will you make to stay faithful to God?

21. Looking at Paul's proclamation at the end of v. 18: When adversity strikes, what is your "proclamation" towards God? Do you search for God's purpose amidst your pain? Or do you usually try and get out of the situation on your own terms? Pray that God will continually help you to respond more like Paul—to be aware of His presence, draw from His strength, and be yielded to His purpose for you.

Think About It: Every time God allows us to be in difficulty, it is a marvelous opportunity to give witness and testimony. The most powerful witness is from people in pain, still walking in faith with Jesus Christ...theirs is the kind of stalwart, courageous witness that shouts and proclaims God is real. (Charles Stanley)

22. From this study, what have you learned about making the choice to live faithfully to your God every day?

Respond to the Lord about what He's shown you today.

Recommended: Listen to "Staying Faithful in View of His Appearing" at melanienewton.com/podcasts after doing this lesson to reinforce what you have learned. Use the listener guide on the next page.

Staying Faithful in View of His Appearing

"In the presence of God and of Christ Jesus, who will judge the living and the dead, and in view of his appearing and his kingdom..." (2 Timothy 4:1)

JESUS' RESURRECTION AND OUR FUTURE LIFE

- Jesus was resurrected from the dead, made appearances to at least 500 followers, then ascended back into heaven. Jesus will one day return. The time between His ascension to heaven and His return to earth is called the "until" time—until His appearing. *Luke 21:24*

- Jesus' Kingdom now is a heaven-initiated kingdom. Every Christian is part of that kingdom. Even now, Jesus has all authority over heaven and earth. *Ephesians 1:21-23*

MOVING OUT

The "until" time is a time of waiting. Lots of believers have died while waiting over the past 2000 years. There isn't much information, but there's enough to provide some clues.

What doesn't happen at death.

- Your soul is not annihilated, disappear, or cease to exist. *Luke 16:19-31; Philippians 1:23*

- Your soul doesn't just sleep or become a floating spirit. You will have conscious enjoyment of the afterlife. *1 Corinthians 15; 2 Corinthians 5:1-10*

- Your soul is not reincarnated into another life form as a second chance to improve your afterlife. You die only once then are judged. *Hebrews 9:27*

- You don't go to purgatory so to be purified to get to heaven. Your immediate entrance into heaven is guaranteed by your faith in Christ. *Colossians 1:22; 2 Corinthians 5:5*

- You don't become an angel. Angels are beings that were made by God at Creation and are entirely different from humans. *Colossians 1:15-17 Hebrews 1:13-14*

What does happen at death

- You fall asleep on earth and wake up in heaven. The Bible teaches no time delay in the transition. *1 Thessalonians 4:14*

- Your soul moves out of this earthly body and is instantly made perfect.

- All Christians who die will receive get a heavenly dwelling fashioned for believers. Then, we will get an immortal body like the one Jesus has. *1 Corinthians 15:35-54; 2 Corinthians 5:8; Philippians 3:20-21; 1 John 3:2*

- You are immediately with the Lord where you can enjoy all the blessings of heaven forever. And we'll finally get to see His face. *Luke 23:43; John 17:24; Philippians 1:23*

MOVING INTO NEW BODIES

- When the "until" time is over, Jesus will appear to complete our new creation. Those who are alive when Jesus comes will be caught up together with those coming with Him from heaven. The phrase "caught up" in Latin is *rapturo* and in English is "rapture." In this event called "The Rapture," Jesus also brings the souls of dead believers with Him, confirming that we are with Him after we die. *1 Thessalonians 4:13-17*

- All believers get to move into new bodies when Jesus comes for us. We shall be changed instantly. God will create a totally new body for each of us to move into. They will be like Jesus' body—human, robust, fully functional, remembering our past and people, yet slightly different in appearance and abilities. Our sin nature will be gone forever! With a perfect body and soul, a permanent indwelling of the Holy Spirit, there will be no capacity for us to sin ever again. *1 Corinthians 15:51-52*

MOVING BACK TO JESUS' KINGDOM ON EARTH

- We'll be moving back here because we will be coming with Jesus (His Second Coming) for the battle against His enemies and staying on to serve Him as King of planet Earth. This Kingdom will last a thousand years (the Millennial Kingdom) with Jerusalem as His capital. All will see His visible Kingdom on the earth. *Revelation 1:5; 17:14; 19:16: 20:4*

- King Jesus will be the King of kings—the supreme political ruler as well as the spiritual leader and object of worship. Righteousness and justice will prevail globally for everyone. There will be worldwide peace among people and even among animals. *Isaiah 11; 65*

- All Christians will move back to earth in our resurrection bodies and participate with Jesus in administering His earthly kingdom. Many natural humans who stayed faithful to God and survived the Tribulation will continue to live in the Kingdom. At the end of the 1000 years according to Revelation 20, Satan will be released from bondage. He'll instigate a rebellion among non-believing people and finally be defeated.

MOVING UP TO GOD'S FOREVER EARTH

- After that time, God will renew the universe and the earth, removing all aspects of sin, and will move His heaven to the renewed earth. God's headquarters will be called the New Jerusalem. This is moving up to God's forever earth—gorgeous and perfect.

- For now, the hope of heaven and the glory of Christ's Kingdom on Earth should transform our perspective on death. Death hurts! But in Christ, we share in His victory over death. We grieve now, but we shouldn't grieve as those who have no hope. We can trust our God to provide grace for us when the time for our death comes.

Let Jesus satisfy your heart with His faithfulness. Then, make the choice to stay faithful to Him for the rest of your life.

Kindle Your Spiritual Gifts

Every believer in Jesus Christ is gifted by the Holy Spirit to serve the Body of Christ. A spiritual gift is a supernatural capacity for service to God in the Body of Christ. All believers receive the same gift of the Holy Spirit but individually receive spiritual gifts that differ, according to the will of God, to be used for the common good.

Although opinions differ on the actual number of spiritual gifts, the Bible clearly indicates a variety of gifts understood from such key passages as Romans 12, 1 Corinthians 12 and Ephesians 4. Listed below are some of the gifts and how they are beneficial to the Body of Christ, especially the local church body.

The following list is adapted from "The Gifts of the Spirit," an article by Kenneth Boa, accessed at www.bible.org.

- **Administration** (1 Corinthians 12:28) — The ability to steer a ministry toward the accomplishment of God-given goals and directives by planning, organizing, and implementing what is needed to accomplish the goal including supervising others. A person may have the gift of leadership without the gift of administration.

- **Discernment** (1 Corinthians 12:10) — The ability to clearly discern the spirit of truth and the spirit of error (cf. 1 John 4:6). With this gift, one can distinguish reality versus counterfeits, the divine versus the demonic, true versus false teaching, and in some cases, spiritual versus carnal motives.

- **Evangelism** (Ephesians 4:11) — The ability to be an unusually effective instrument in leading unbelievers to a saving knowledge of Christ. Some with this gift are most effective in personal evangelism, while others may be used by God in group evangelism or cross-cultural evangelism.

- **Exhortation** (Romans 12:8) — The ability to motivate others to respond to the truth by providing timely words of counsel, encouragement, and consolation. When this gift is exercised, believers are challenged to stimulate their faith by putting God's truth to the test in their lives.

- **Faith** (1 Corinthians 12:9) — The ability to have a vision for what God wants to be done and to confidently believe that it will be accomplished in spite of circumstances and appearances to the contrary. The gift of faith transforms vision into reality.

- **Giving** (Romans 12:8) — The ability to contribute material resources with generosity and cheerfulness for the benefit of others and the glory of God. Christians with this spiritual gift need not be wealthy.

- **Helps** (1 Corinthians 12:28) — The ability to enhance the effectiveness of the ministry of other members of the body. Some suggest that while the gift of service is more group-oriented, the gift of helps is more person-oriented.

- **Leadership** (Romans 12:8) — The ability to discern God's purpose for a group, set and communicate appropriate goals, and motivate others to work together to fulfill them in the service of God. A person with this gift is effective at delegating tasks to followers without manipulation or coercion.

- **Mercy** (Romans 12:8) — The ability to deeply empathize and engage in compassionate acts on behalf of people who are suffering physical, mental, or emotional distress. Those with this gift manifest concern and kindness to people who are often overlooked.

- **Service** (Romans 12:7) — The ability to identify and care for the physical needs of the body through a variety of means.

- **Shepherd or pastor** (Ephesians 4:11) — A person with this spiritual gift has the ability to personally lead, nourish, protect, and care for the needs of a group of believers. Many with this gift do not have or need the office of pastor to be useful to the body.

- **Teaching** (Romans 12:7; 1 Corinthians 12:28-29; Ephesians 4:11) — The ability to clearly explain and effectively apply the truths of God's Word so that others will learn. This requires the capacity to accurately interpret Scripture, engage in necessary research, and organize the results in a way that is easily communicated.

- **Wisdom** (1 Corinthians 12:8) — The ability to apply the principles of the Word of God in a practical way to specific situations and to recommend the best course of action at the best time. The exercise of this gift skillfully distills insight and discernment into excellent advice.

Discover Your Spiritual Giftedness

Various spiritual gift assessments are available to further help you understand how you have been gifted. We recommend the online spiritual gifts analysis freely provided by "Ephesians Four Ministries" of the Church Growth Institute at the following website: www.churchgrowth.org. Allow yourself at least 15 minutes to take this assessment (or any other assessment you have available to you). At the end, you will receive a detailed description of what may be your main spiritual gift. Often, a second gift is evident, and that description will be displayed as well. If possible, print these descriptions for future reference.

Primary gift: _____

Secondary gift (if applicable): _____

What did you discover about yourself regarding your spiritual gift(s) and how they could benefit your local community of believers?

Small Group Discussion Guide

The following guide is designed for groups that meet for about 1½ hours or less. You will notice that some questions are skipped for the sake of time. These are only suggestions for you.

IF YOU HAVE A SEPARATE WEEK TO INTRODUCE THE STUDY:

- *Ask the group to listen to the first podcast "Staying Faithful to God by Choice" before coming to the first meeting.* Send them a link to melanienewton.com/podcasts. Go to Series 11: 2 Timothy.

Introduce the study

- Start with prayer. Pray for the group to learn from Jesus what He wants them to know and to learn to love one another well to build our community.

- Make sure everyone has a book, a schedule, and Bible / Bible app and knows how to use it. Ask if anyone is new to the Bible and plan to come alongside her during the week.

- Get acquainted with each other. Ask a general question or two such as, "Share your name, where you live, and an activity you enjoy when you have time to do so."

- **Pray:** Ask Jesus to teach you through this semester what He wants you to know. Ask Him to help you learn how to rely on Him more than on yourselves every day.

- **Introduction on Page 1**. Read the top paragraphs and "The Basic Study" section. Draw their attention to the useful study tools at the bottom of the page. Tell them how to find the podcasts (melanienewton.com/2-timothy or any podcast platform—search "Satisfied" by Melanie Newton, Season 11). Or you can read the blogs associated with the podcasts at melanienewton.com/blog. Choose 2 Timothy category then scroll to find the title you want.

- **Look at Lesson 2** to illustrate how the lesson is arranged. Every study day begins and ends in prayer. Day One Study is always observation of the whole passage. You get to mark anything that grabs your attention, thoughts that connect, and anything you think relates to being faithful. You also get to choose a verse upon which to dwell for the week.

- **Back to page 2**: Read "New Testament Summary" or suggest they do so on their own.

- Read "Discussion Group Guidelines." Add anything else pertinent to your group.

- **Staying Faithful to God by Choice Podcast:** Read and discuss the listener guide on pages 7-8. Ask questions and add insights based on your notes from listening to the podcast ahead of time.

- Tell them to work on Lesson One for the next meeting.

- Share prayer requests and pray for one another.

Recommendation: Listen to a worship song such as "Lord, I Need You."

LESSON 1: TRUTH AND FAITHFULNESS

Choose ahead of time which verses from the questions the group will read aloud as you proceed through the discussion. My recommendations are below.

Start with prayer.

- If you have not already discussed "Staying Faithful to God by Choice" podcast, do so here. See suggestions above.

Day One Study

- Choose whether or not to read the ABC's. Ask Q1.
- Pray then read paragraphs under "Get the Big Picture."
- Ask Q2.

Day Two Study

- Ask Q3.
- Q4: Read the verses.
- Ask Q5.

Day Three Study

- Qs6 & 7: Read the verses.
- Ask Q8.
- Ask Q9.
- Read "What does it mean to "Stay Faithful?" Read "Focus on the Meaning."

Podcast and More

- Ask what grabbed their attention from the podcast. Highlight what you want to emphasize.
- Pray.

Recommendation: Listen to a worship song such as "Build My Life."

LESSON 2: STAY FAITHFUL WITHOUT FEAR

Choose ahead of time which verses from the questions the group will read aloud as you proceed through the discussion. My recommendations are below.

Start with prayer.

Day One Study

- Read 2 Timothy 1:1-7. Ask Qs1-5.

Day Two Study

- Read "Historical Insight."
- Ask Qs6-9.
- Read "Historical Insight."
- Ask Q11.

Day Three Study

- Q12: Read the verses. Read "From the Greek."
- Q13: Read 1 Corinthians 16:10 and 1 Timothy 4:12.
- Read "From the Greek."
- Qs14 & 15: Read the verses.
- Qs16 & 17.

Podcast and More

- Ask what grabbed their attention from the podcast. Highlight what you want to emphasize.
- Read and discuss "A Process to Apply Faith to Any Fear."
- Pray.

Recommendation: Listen to a worship song such as "Whom Shall I Fear."

LESSON 3: FAITHFULNESS WITHOUT SHAME

Choose ahead of time which verses from the questions the group will read aloud as you proceed through the discussion. My recommendations are below.

Start with prayer.

Day One Study

- Read 2 Timothy 1:7-18. Qs1-5.

Day Two Study

- Skip reading passage if you did it already. Read "Historical Insight."
- Q6. Read "Focus on the Meaning."
- Qs7-8. Read "Historical Insight."
- Q9: Read verses.
- Q10. Skip "Scriptural Insight."
- Q11. Read "Think About It."
- Q12. Read "Dependent Living."
- Q13: Read vv. 13-14 but not the others. Read "Dependent Living."
- Q14.

Day Three Study

- Q15. Read "Focus on the Meaning."
- Qs16-17.
- Q18: Read the verses.
- Q19. Read "Historical Insight."
- Qs20-21.
- Q22 is personal, but you can ask whom they chose and why.

Podcast and More

- Ask what grabbed their attention from the podcast. Highlight what you want to emphasize, especially the sections "Substitute Treasure Is Worthless" and "Jesus Christ is more powerful than any substitute."
- Pray.

Recommendation: Listen to a worship song such as "In Christ Alone."

LESSON 4: THE HARD WORK OF FAITHFULNESS

Choose ahead of time which verses from the questions the group will read aloud as you proceed through the discussion. My recommendations are below.

Start with prayer.

Day One Study

- Read 2 Timothy 2:1-13 and "From the Greek." Qs1-5.

Day Two Study

- Skip reading passage if you did it already. Read third paragraph under "What does it mean?"
- Qs6-7. Read "Dependent Living."
- Q8. Skip "Focus on the Meaning."
- Q9. Read "Think About It."
- Qs10-12. Read "Historical Insight."
- Q13. Read "Focus on the Meaning."
- Qs14-15. Skip "Focus on the Meaning."
- Q16.
- Skip Q17. Ask Q18.

Day Three Study

- Q19. Read "Historical Insight."
- Read paragraphs under "A popular saying."
- Q20. Read "Focus on the Meaning."
- Q21. Read Luke 22:31-34. Read "Focus on the Meaning."
- Q22.
- Q23.

Podcast and More

- Ask what grabbed their attention from the podcast. Highlight what you want to emphasize.
- Pray.

Recommendation: Listen to a worship song such as "Lord, I Need You."

LESSON 5: FAITH-BUILDING WORDS

Choose ahead of time which verses from the questions the group will read aloud as you proceed through the discussion. My recommendations are below.

Start with prayer.

Day One Study

- Read 2 Timothy 2:14-26. Qs1-5.

Day Two Study

- Read 2 Timothy 2:2-6. Skip reading verses 14-26 if you did it already.

- Read paragraph.

- Q6 and "From the Greek."

- Qs7-8. Read "Think About It."

- Q9. Read "From the Greek."

- Qs10-11.

Day Three Study

- Qs12-14.

- Q15. Read "Scriptural Insight."

- Qs16-17. Read "Focus on the Meaning."

- Qs18-19.

- Qs20-21.

Podcast and More

- Ask what grabbed their attention from the podcast. Highlight what you want to emphasize. The use of our words is a huge issue for us to grasp.

- Pray.

Recommendation: Listen to a worship song such as "Build My Life."

LESSON 6: INFLUENTIAL FAKERS

Choose ahead of time which verses from the questions the group will read aloud as you proceed through the discussion. My recommendations are below.

Start with prayer.

Day One Study

- Read 2 Timothy 3:1-13. Qs1-5.

Day Two Study

- Skip reading passage if you did it already. Read paragraph under "What does it mean?"
- Q6. Read "Dependent Living."
- Q7: Read Acts 20:28-31 and Titus 1:16.
- Q8.
- Q9. Read "Focus on the Meaning."
- Q10. Read "Focus on the Meaning."
- Qs11-13. Skip "Scriptural Insight."
- Qs14-15. Skip Q16 (personal).

Day Three Study

- Qs17-18. Skip "Scriptural Insight."
- Q19. Read "Scriptural Insight."
- Q20. Read 2 Corinthians 1:9; 4:7-9; and 12:9-10. Read "Dependent Living."
- Q21.
- Discuss "Dangerous Times for Christians" section.

Podcast and More

- Ask what grabbed their attention from the podcast. Highlight what you want to emphasize. Remind them how important it is to grasp biblical truth as a protection from being taken captive by worldly influences.
- Pray.

Recommendation: Listen to a worship song such as "Lord, I Need You."

LESSON 7: A FAITHFUL LIFE WITH NO REGRETS

Choose ahead of time which verses from the questions the group will read aloud as you proceed through the discussion. My recommendations are below.

Start with prayer.

Day One Study

- Read 2 Timothy 3:14-4:8. Qs1-5.

Day Two Study

- Skip reading passage if you did it already. Qs6-7.
- Q8. Read all the verses referenced and "Focus on the Meaning."
- Qs9-10. Read Romans 15:4.
- Q11. Read 2 Timothy 4:1-2, 8. Read "Historical Insight."
- Q12. Read "Focus on the Meaning."
- Qs13-14.
- Qs15-16.

Day Three Study

- Read 2 Timothy 4:3-5. Q17 and "Focus on the Meaning."
- Q18. Read the verses.
- Qs19-21.
- Q22. Read 2 Timothy 4:6-8. Read "Scriptural Insight."
- Q23. Read "Dependent Living."
- Q24. Read "Scriptural Insight."
- Qs25-26.

Podcast and More

- Ask what grabbed their attention from the podcast. Highlight what you want to emphasize.
- Pray.

> Recommendation: Listen to a worship song such as "Abide."

LESSON 8: STAY FAITHFUL TO THE END

Choose ahead of time which verses from the questions the group will read aloud as you proceed through the discussion. My recommendations are below.

Start with prayer.

Day One Study

- Read 2 Timothy 4:9-22. Qs1-5.

Day Two Study

- Skip reading passage if you did it already.
- Q6. Read "Historical Insight."
- Q7. Read Philemon 24. Skip "Focus on the Meaning."
- Q8. Skip "Historical Insight."
- Q9. Read verses.
- Q10. Read "Historical Insight."
- Q11. Read "Focus on the Meaning."

Day Three Study

- Read 2 Timothy 4:16-22.
- Read "From the Greek." Q12.
- Qs13-14.
- Q15. Read verses.
- Q16. Read "Focus on the Meaning."
- Qs17-18.
- Q19. Read Acts 18:2-3. Skip other verses unless you have time. Read "Historical Insight."
- Q20.
- Q21. Read "Think About It."
- Q22.

Podcast and More

- Ask what grabbed their attention from the podcast. Highlight what you want to emphasize. Read theme statement together at the end of the listener guide.
- Pray.

Recommendation: Listen to a worship song such as "Build My Life."

Sources

1. *2 Timothy Life Change Bible Study*
2. Charles Stanley quote
3. John Foxe, *Foxe's Book of Martyrs*
4. John Stott, *Bible Study Guide on 2 Timothy*
5. *Life Application Bible Commentary, 1 & 2 Timothy & Titus*
6. *The Word in Life Study Bible*
7. Tim Stevenson, Mind Games sermon notes

www.ingramcontent.com/pod-product-compliance
Lightning Source LLC
Chambersburg PA
CBHW080752120626
46557CB00005B/1238